A BURNING DESIRE TO WIN

Ray and Sandy;
    The highlight of coaching
at U.T. was being on the
Coaching staff with you * I
always considered you a great
Coach. I also enjoy being
on the sports Page to hear
your down to earth comments.
        Thanks.
        Lonnie

A BURNING DESIRE TO WIN

"Run with champions, you become a champion"

Lon (Lonnie) Herzbrun

ISBN 13: 978-1516987931

ISBN 10: 1516987934

Special thanks to Terry Lindsay,
a lifetime friend of Lonnie,
who provided the photograph and captions for the back cover.

First Edition, printed in the United States of America

2015

G

GJ Publishing
515 Cimarron Circle, Suite 323
Loudon, Tennessee 37774
865-458-1355
www.neilans.com
booksbyneilans@aol.com

DEDICATION

This book is dedicated to my deceased family members: my mom Tina, my father Edward and my two brothers Philip and Joseph. They all set the bar high with their many accomplishments and their shown love for our family members. Also, to my children's mother Wilma and my children and their families: Eric, his wife Jan and their children, Lee and Alicia, and my daughter Yvette and her husband Harold Smiddy. I also have a special admiration for Wilma's deceased parents: her mom Stelma Brown, and her dad Carie Brown. Both of them were very bright and hardworking. They were brought up in country and mountain environments in Tennessee. Stelma raised and killed farm animals and grew home grown vegetables for cooking delicious country style meals. She was also very artistic, making pottery and decorations in her own kiln. Carie, who was brought up in the unique, beautiful Cades Cove mountainous area, learned hard work and how to make decisions in order to survive in this secluded mountainous setting. Finally, to my own coaches, teammates, coaches I coached with, and the many players I had the pleasure of coaching. All of these people paid the price to achieve greatness in their respective fields of endeavor. All are champions because they have learned to prepare and finish.

PREFACE AND ACKNOWLEDGEMENTS

I have always questioned where my burning desire to win came from. I did not have a lot of natural physical abilities. My height was at best 5' 9 ¾". I had an average speed and jumping ability, but I did have two important physical assets: natural strength and quickness.

My thoughts are: if you RUN WITH CHAMPIONS, YOU BECOME A CHAMPION. I had great leaders, family members, coaches, and teammates throughout my career who all had the same desires to win.

I had the privilege of playing on many championship teams in different sports and in different stages of my life. I'm aware that one man on a team does not win championships by himself. I personally have always believed the greatest attribute an athlete can have is confidence, which can only be gained through repetition and by paying the price in practices in order to be a winner on game day. I never went into a contest thinking that we wouldn't win. Throughout my life, particularly in sports, I put myself in a position to make something happen in order to win. I am now eighty years old, and this book may be my last hurrah.

I will forever be grateful to Kayla and Renae Lewis who put in many hours editing, proofing, and typing all of my scribbling.

To be successful isn't what you do, but how and with whom you do it. I feel with the steadfastness of Kayla and Renae that this book has a chance to be successful.

I also want to note my appreciation to Joyce Gurley for her expertise in correcting my grammar in the manuscript of this book.

A special thanks to Herb Newton for his support and encouragement.

CONTENTS

1ˢᵗ QUARTER

ROOTS

My grandfather, Josef Herzbrun, was born in Hungary in the mid 1800's. He was Jewish, and at that time many Jews were leaving Hungary because they were being persecuted. A large group of ancestral Herzbruns, including my grandfather Josef, left Hungary and arrived in New York City in the late 1800's. My grandfather met his wife, Lena Helfgott, who was also a Jew from Hungary, in New York City when she arrived with her family in 1879. They were married in 1884 in New York.

In the early 1900's, members of the Welch, West Virginia City Council came to New York City soliciting my grandfather, who was a tailor by trade, because they needed a tailor. My grandparents then moved to Welch. They were the second Jewish family in that town. Welch, West Virginia is the seat of McDowell County (population of approximately 4,000). It is known as the quintessence of Appalachia. It is rich in coal and poor people. Welch was the birthplace of the federal food stamp program.

The town is approximately one mile long with steep mountains surrounding it. It is located in a narrow valley with the Tug River flowing through the center. It is also known to have the first municipality owned parking lot in the United States. The mountains are a problem; but as a resident once said, "How many places do you know where you can stand at the basement door and spit on the roof of a three-story house?" There are also miles of coal mines that run under the city. There was a tradition in the mining towns: when the miners came out of the mines, they had coal dust in their throats and lungs, which could cause a disease called Black Lung. So at every meal, there was a plate of hot peppers that the miners would eat before the actual meal to cut the coal dust in their throats. My family followed this tradition because it was so common in the area, even though we did not work in the mines.

McDowell County is the most rugged county east of the Rockies. There are no farms in the entire county. It was much like the Wild West. Most of the men in McDonnell County carried holstered guns. My father carried his gun in a shoulder holster. Almost all of the families had rifles. There were feuds, and the most notable was the Hatfield's from West Virginia and the McCoy's from Kentucky.

There was also a war going on between the coal companies and people who wanted to unionize the miners. The union brought in the Baldwin Felts detectives to fight for their side of the war. My mother, Tina Herzbrun remembered the time when she was walking down the courthouse steps in Welch in 1921 when a Baldwin Felts detective shot and killed Sid Hatfield and Ed Chambers. They fell dead right there at her feet. She screamed ... and never forgot that horrific historical event.

The miners were paid in scrip and could only use this play money in company stores, but there were places in Welch that would pay the miners $0.60 for each dollar of scrip.

The miners made nothing and lived from one paycheck to another.

My grandfather, Josef, eventually became director of the First National Bank and a member of the Welch City Council. His wife, Lena, had four children: my father Edward born in 1895 in New York, his brother Maurice and sisters Anna and Ruth. My father met his wife Tina Marjulies, from Baltimore, Maryland in Welch while she was visiting her sister Goldie and Goldie's husband Hymie Siff. My mom and dad were married in 1922 in Baltimore, Maryland, and then moved back to live in Welch.

My dad worked with my grandfather in the tailor shop. The sign on the shop was eventually J. Herzbrun and Sons.

Welch, West Virginia

My dad was intelligent. He attended West Virginia University for two years to be a lawyer. He never graduated, but his brother became a lawyer. Dad was on Welch's City Council from 1927 to 1935, until the family moved to Washington, D.C.

He was an honorary 33rd Degree Mason. I understood there were very few 33rd Degree Masons awarded.

Later on in my life while I was playing for the Washington Redskins, I was sitting in a bar in a bowling alley in Los Angeles, where the Redskins had their pre-season football camp. When several of the team players were sitting on one side of me, a girl came in and sat on the other side. She struck up a conversation by asking what kind of ring I was wearing. The ring was my father's **Masons** ring, which I wore as my wedding ring. This was okay to wear, as my dad had passed away. I said to her, "That's a **Masons** ring," and she said, "My father was a **carpenter**." The ball players on the other side of me laughed out loud. I didn't know what to say to her and no further conversation took place.

My dad was quick-witted and outspoken and had a good sense of humor. He was very talented as an artist. He would draw many pictures with a pencil and could also scribe fancy lettering, but never pursued it any further. He was very good at billiards, a game he learned to play in his early years in New York City and Welch. He spent much of his time playing billiards in the Elks Lodge. He would go back and forth from Welch to New York, staying with cousins, playing billiards and probably betting on his game.

Later when we moved to Washington, D.C., he was an insurance agent with the Life Insurance Company of Virginia. In D.C., I went several times with him to the Elks Lodge, where he

4

would supplement his insurance agent salary by winning at billiards.

Dad was short in statue with huge calves. The only thing he did physically other than billiards was setting a complete dining room table with dishes, silverware, and drinking glasses by walking on his hands on the top of the table. Mom said he was a show-off and a playboy. He died at the age of 63.

My mom, Tina Herzbrun, was the strength of the family. She was a gourmet cook and did the laundry, housekeeping, and gardening. She basically raised us three boys. We never had a car in D.C., so mom would walk over a half mile to do our grocery shopping. I could have counted on one hand the times our family went out to a restaurant to eat.

Later on, after my brothers left home and I was in junior high and high school, Mom worked part-time for her step-sister Elsie and her husband Mort Blum in a jewelry and cosmetic store in Alexandria, Virginia. She would take one bus in D.C. and transfer to another bus to go to Alexandria, approximately thirty miles from our home.

Still later, after I went to college, Mom worked full time. Sometimes she managed the whole store when my aunt and uncle were on vacation.

Mom was a strict disciplinarian. She used a coiled rubber strap on us boys, and we were never allowed to move while taking the beating. We always deserved the beatings we got. She was a stocky, small, beautiful woman. Mom's dad was an opera singer and my mom had some operatic training. When Mom would call me from the neighborhood to come home, I could hear her hollering, "Lonnie," from two blocks away. She said her hair turned silver, not grey, when she was in her early 30's. She blamed the premature silver on her three sons. It was that color silver until she died at the age of 89.

My parents kept the Jewish high holidays in our home. They spoke the customary prayers at the dinner meals in Yiddish, a High German dialect. Mother also prepared the traditional meals during those holidays.

There were reasons why we could not attend the synagogue during these holidays. There was only one temple in D.C. and it was fifteen miles from our house and we didn't have a car. Another reason was the cost to buy a seat in the temple, which we could not afford.

MY BROTHERS

My two brothers and I were born in Welch, West Virginia. Philip (Phil), the oldest, was born in 1924. My brother Joseph (Joe) was born in 1928. I was born in 1934.

Joe, Lonnie, Phil

7

My grandfather, Josef Herzbrun, had died in 1927, and my grandmother died the year I was born.

We moved from Welch to D.C. for many reasons. First of all, the family tailor shop failed ... mainly because of the Great Depression. Both of my dad's parents had died. My dad always enjoyed the big city life since he had been brought up in New York City.

Another reason we left Welch was that my mom's family lived in surrounding towns of D.C. Her mom, Jennie and Jennie's daughter, Rose, lived in Baltimore, Maryland, and my mom's step-sister, Elsie, lived in Alexandria, Virginia. Another one of my mom's sisters, Goldie and her husband Hymie Siff, lived in D.C. The Siff's had moved from Welch to D.C. several years prior to our moving. Hymie had a job working at the Hecht Department Store and informed my dad there was a job opening at that store in the men's clothing department. As Dad had worked as a tailor in Welch, he knew clothing. My dad took the job at the Hecht Department Store and later he became an insurance agent with the Life Insurance Company of Virginia.

We left Welch during 1935 in a nearly broken down car. It was a Hupmobile; the doors were tied shut with rope, and in order to get out, we had to untie the doors. This was the last car we had after arriving in D.C.

All three of us boys took different paths in life. Phil, my oldest brother, took the academic route. Joe, the middle brother, took the artistic route. I, the youngest, took the athletic route. All of us became highly successful in our chosen fields. You have to love what you are doing to put in the required time it takes to reach the greatest success. I was never very close to my brothers because of the age difference, but I looked up to them because of their accomplishments. One thing the three of us had in common was we became perfectionists at whatever we liked doing. We all become highly competitive to be the best.

Phil was a genius with an I.Q. of 185. In 1933, at the age of nine, he was a pianist and won the West Virginia State Music Contest. When he was three years old, he pushed a screen from a second-story window at our house and fell out with it. The screen landed on some telephone wires with Phil on top. Unhurt, he was soon rescued from the perilous position by my mom. This incident was depicted in a widely published newspaper cartoon years later.

Phil's early education was in Welch. When we arrived in D.C. in 1935, he attended Paul Junior High School and then went to Roosevelt High School. There was an article about Phil in a newspaper, *The Junior Star* on May 12, 1940. The article read, "Jack-of-All-Trades is a title that might well apply to Philip Herzbrun, 16, of Roosevelt High School. Although he intends to limit his career to writing, Phil is proficient in other arts including music, sketching, dancing, singing, and writing poetry."

Following his ambition to be an author, while a junior at Roosevelt High, he had one story accepted by Liberty Magazine, which brought him $18, and another one of his short stories, "All Is Fair," along with his poem, "Of Superstitions, Old and New" were printed in the school paper.

In 1936, the versatile youth made his dancing debut in a Russian ballet with the civic theater in D.C. Honorable Mention in a scholastic contest was the result of another of his talents: sketching.

In addition to writing, Phil was active in the music field. He played the glockenspiel in the Roosevelt Band and the Washington

Redskins Football Band. He played the piano in the high school swing orchestra; he also appreciated classical music.

Phil was also a member of the Boy's Glee Club at Roosevelt and an active member in sports teams. He played center on the football team, first base on the baseball team, and was a distance runner in track.

Phil held the mile record on the East Coast in 1940. His time was 4:36.4. At the time Roger Bannister hadn't broken the four-minute mile, but I have Phil's trophy with the time mistakenly engraved on it as 3:36.4. Phil, later in his life after the four-minute record had been broken, commented, "They're getting close to my record."

At Roosevelt High School, Phil took both Latin and Spanish, which served him well later in his career of teaching English. He also read and knew the Bible through the Latin version. He later taught Spanish at night. His pupils were U. S. cabinet members' wives taking primer Spanish.

After graduating from high school, he joined the Armed Forces in 1942. While in the Navy, he served with Gene Kelly who later became a well-known dancer, singer, and movie star. Phil said that he had once loaned Gene some money that was never paid back.

Phil got a scholarship to George Washington University, where he received his Bachelors and Master's Degrees. In 1946, he became a member of Phi Beta Kappa. While at George Washington, Phil played the piano in the top nightclubs and with traveling bands along the East Coast, and spent summers playing on cruise ships. Phil had his own band called "The Hartwells." He also received a scholarship to Johns Hopkins where they eventually gifted him a doctorate's degree in English. The professors said Phil knew more than they did.

Phil loved to teach. He taught English, first at George Washington University in Washington D.C., then later at Georgetown University in Washington D.C. When he was teaching at George Washington University, he had Jacqueline Bouvier as one of his students. She later became the wife of President John F. Kennedy and the first lady. When he was teaching at Georgetown, he also taught Patrick Ewing, a great college and professional basketball player.

Phil's first wife, Nancy, wanted Phil to make more money. The government offered him a large salary because of his brain and knowledge of the English language. The government Bureau of Standards recruited him to put in the English language for the first computers. He loved teaching at Georgetown, but because of his wife, he accepted the new job.

After I had just gotten married in Tennessee, to Wilma Brown from Alcoa, Tennessee, I brought her to Washington, D.C to my house to introduce her to my mom and dad, and my brother and his wife. We were all gathered in the living room conversing when Nancy, my brother's wife, was explaining the Bureau of Standards' asking Phil to work for them. She said they offered him a lot more money than teaching at Georgetown University. My dad knew how much Phil loved teaching and so he said to her, "You could make a lot more money on your back." Nancy left and went upstairs for the duration of the evening. My new wife, Wilma, was shocked. She didn't know my dad always expressed whatever he thought.

When Phil eventually divorced Nancy, he went back to Georgetown University, teaching English and reviewing poetry for

11

what was then *The Sunday Washington Star*. I once asked him why he was a poet critic, yet I never saw a negative review he had written. His answer was that he didn't want to discourage a young writer with just his personal opinion.

Phil married Helene McKinney, who was an accomplished abstract artist and later became the head of the art department at American University in Washington, D.C. One time my wife Wilma and I visited Phil and Helene who were playing their weekly volleyball game with their Sunday group of intellectual friends. Wilma and I were introduced to Doug Wallope, who wrote the book, *The Day the Yankees Lost the Pennant,* and he said that they were going to make it into a play on Broadway, but they didn't have a name for it. Phil suggested they call it the "Damn Yankees," which later became the Broadway show's name. Doug's wife, Lucille Fletcher, wrote the great novel "Sorry, Wrong Number." Another couple we met at this Sunday volleyball game was newscaster David Brinkley and his wife.

Phil became like another father to me, perhaps because of the age difference and his interest in my athletic career. He kept scrapbooks of newspaper clippings from my high school days all the way through my coaching career. The most significant thing I could remember of Phil was that he could get on anyone's mental level. He never bragged but he had great knowledge on almost every subject. He was a walking encyclopedia. Phil died in 1995 at the age of 71.

My brother Joe Herzbrun, who later changed his name to Joseph Erhardy, was born in 1928. He was six years older than I. He was greatly influenced by Phil, who was four years older. In Welch, we had a community swimming pool not far from our house. At a very early age, Joe kept doing all sorts of high-dives, front and back flips, and twists from the high diving board. He couldn't swim so my oldest brother, Phil, would dive into the water and rescue him to the side of the pool. Joe continued this act of making Phil bring him to the side of the pool over and over.

Later during Joe's high school days at Wilson High, he won the Junior Olympics in a diving contest. He became interested in drawing and painting at Wilson High School. He painted four stained glass windows, twelve-feet high, on canvas, which the school brought out on the stage every Easter during assembly, even six years later when I attended Wilson High.

Sometime during his high school days, Joe converted to the Catholic religion. My family never knew; I just happened to find his rosary in his desk in the bedroom. D.C. was predominately Catholic, so all his friends were Catholic.

He took art lessons at Corcoran School of Arts. He was drawing nude models. My dad asked Joe, "Was it 'hard' to draw the nude models?" Joe stated, "It was 'hard' at first." Joe later got large stones, mostly granite, in the vicinity of D.C., and sculpted them into heads and figures using regular chisels and a hammer.

He brought home two large soapstones that were found in the Rock Creek Park in D.C. He sculpted a nude woman out of one of them, which he set on the kitchen table to admire. I was making sandwiches while Mom was at work and accidently flung mayonnaise on the statue. Joe knocked me across the kitchen. When he went to rub the mayonnaise off the statue, it began to shine. He then rubbed the whole jar of mayonnaise on the statue. When Mom came home the mayonnaise had started to smell sour. She put the statue on the back porch, where it remained for years.

When Joe went to Europe on a scholarship, my oldest brother put a wooden base on the statue and put it in his house. When Phil died, I inherited the statue. It is now in my house and still shines even though nothing else was ever put on it. The other soapstone, which was a sculptured head, is also in my front yard along with several other statues made from granite.

Mayonnaise for luster

Joe learned to play drums and timpani while in high school. He played both in the school orchestra and with the Washington Symphony Orchestra. He was one of the best drummers in dance bands throughout the Washington area. He played in the top nightclubs in the area. He also had his own band and named it the same as Phil's band, "The Hartwells."

Joe was always fascinated by guns. Mom would make him take me to Temple on Saturday mornings in downtown D.C., but we never made it to the Temple. We went through every pawnshop in downtown D.C. looking at guns. Joe had money from playing the drums in the nightclubs.

When I was very young, Mom would make Joe take me with him. One time, I was with him when he carried a tripod machine gun, wrapped in a raincoat. We took a streetcar down to the Potomac River, D.C. side. He left me in the woods. He then rented a canoe further down the river, launched the boat and carried the machine gun to the middle of the river. He then mounted the gun to the middle of the canoe and commenced firing at the cliffs on the Virginia side. The canoe turned over with the machine gun; it sank in the river. I saw everything from the D.C. riverbank; and then came the cops. I hid from them in the woods, scared to death. In the meantime, Joe swam to the Virginia side of the river. I was left in the woods until it got dark and the police had gone. I couldn't leave because I was too young to know where I was, and I had no money to take the street car back home. Joe finally came through the woods where he had left me, calling, "Lonnie, where are you?" We never mentioned it to Mom, or it would have meant a beating for both of us.

Another time, I was walking our big Doberman Pinscher, which was actually Joe's dog, in the woods near our house. I had a next door neighbor who later became a pitcher in baseball, and I played catcher on the team with him at Wilson High. He came with me to walk the dog in the woods.

Joe showed up with a small caliber pistol with a hair trigger. The gun accidently went off, and the bullet went through Joe's hand into the thigh of the neighbor. My brother, who was of small stature but was very muscular, carried the 6'1", approximately 150-pound neighbor three blocks to his home. Of course, his parents weren't too happy.

Both my brother and my neighbor survived with no after effects.

Many years later, after Joe was in Europe, those same neighbors sent a petition to get us out of the neighborhood because we were Jewish. Nobody signed the petition, except for the neighbor next door who had started it. The neighbors on the other side of our house brought the unsigned petition to show to Mom.

My mom was a gourmet cook, and she cooked some Jewish and other ethnic foods many times for the neighbors, including the neighbors who had sent out the petition. I actually think they were jealous of the three of us boys getting a lot of attention for all of our accomplishments in the Washington newspapers.

After high school, Joe enlisted in the Army-Air Force Band. Somehow, when he enlisted, he also enlisted his well-trained Doberman Pinscher to go with him. The dog was trained to parade in front of the band with white crossing straps across his chest as his uniform.

After service, he came home and attended George Washington University for a quarter, and continued his sculpting. He sculpted out of granite a six-foot dead soldier, who had a hand

and foot missing. With this statue, he won a national prestigious award, The Times Harold Art Show Award, which gave him a scholarship to study in Italy.

After winning the scholarship award, he didn't like the statue, so he was going to bury the dead granite soldier and insisted it had to be buried six feet deep. He enlisted me to help him bury it in the woods near our house. Much later, they were building a Lord and Taylor department store on this property. I was waiting for the comments to be made when they unburied the statue. It turned out the parking lot was put over the area of the statue, and they didn't excavate that part six feet deep where it lay. To this day, the statue is still buried there.

Joe left the U.S. in 1949. I am not sure when he changed his name to Joseph Erhardy from Josef Herzbrun. He studied under the scholarship in Florence, Italy in 1949 at the Academia di Belle Arti. He then lived in Rome until 1952, when he enrolled in de la Grand Chaumière in Paris, where he met his wife Melanie Van Muyden from Holland, an established artist in her own right. They had three sons, four daughters, and seven grandchildren.

Joe's works are displayed throughout Europe, France, Great Britain, Italy, and the Netherlands. He was considered one of the most well-known sculptors in Europe and the U.S.

Some of Joe's notable pieces of work are:

- "Warriors Head" marble. The Corcoran Gallery of Art, D. C. (acquired in 1962)
- "Bather" marble, "Little Flower" marble, "Little Head" marble, The Josef H. Hishorn Museum and Sculpture Garden, Washington, D.C. (acquired in 1964)
- "John Kenneth Galbraith" marble portrait bust, the National Portrait Gallery, Washington, D.C. (acquired in 1981)
- "Daniel Boorstin," Library of Congress, bronze portrait bust. The Library of Congress, Washington, D.C. (acquired in 1983)
- M.I.T. Museum "Sir Robert Jackson," low relief

Some Notable Museums in Europe that have some of Joe's pieces:
- Vatican Museum, the Vatican Rome, Italy. "Crucifix"
- Pompidou Centre/Beaubourg, Paris, France
- Downing College, University of Cambridge, UK
  Beelden aan Zee, The Netherlands (bronze) 1955

The most impressive work Joe sculpted is a twelve-foot high and twelve-foot long statue of the Calvary scene with six figures. It is called "The Mystery of Salvation." A theologian, Sabine de Lavergne of France, writes the description of Joe's statue:

"Joseph Erhardy's imposing Calvary is a challenging message for the end of the 20th century. Today, a six-figure group, four metres high and almost as large, in a style at once classically French and contemporary, evokes both attention and respect.

"The total simplicity of this work appeals to the eye and invites reflection. One would like to discover it on a hill, in a harmonious landscape where it would be seen by people in search of spiritual refreshment or simply keen to experience the silent gravity emanating from such a sculpture.

"When speaking of Erhardy, Jean Clair states that, 'If his previous sculptures could appear ill-timed in an epoch of "sound and fury", how very much stranger to contemporary eyes will appear his only religious sculpture, in which six figures represent the timeless drama of the Christian Mystery.'

"Thus Joseph Erhardy himself bears witness. A timeless appeal in favour of Hope and contemplative silence, his great Calvary is an admirable challenge in this age of insecurity and anxiety."

Sabine de Lavergne, Docteur en theologie et historienne d'art

June 1, 2000

The Mystery Of Salvation

Henri Cartier-Bresson, world renowned photographer, put a photo portrait of Joseph Erhardy in his book *Henri Cartier-Bresson Photoportraits* in 1985, with such notables as Isaac Stern, The Duke and Duchess of Windsor, Pablo Picasso, Leonard Bernstein, Gandhi, and Harry S. Truman.

Joseph Erhardy died in 2012 in Paris, France.

Joe with sculpted head of daughter

2nd QUARTER

ELEMENTARY SCHOOL

I was one year old when our family came to D.C. in 1935. We lived in a small bungalow in Northwest D.C., in the neighborhood of Roosevelt High School.

My first impression of sports was when my oldest brother, Phil, played center on the Roosevelt High School football team. He took me to a football scrimmage with him when I was only seven years old, and had me carry some sliced oranges, wrapped in wax paper, for him. When the team took a water break, he would come over to me and take a couple of the orange slices that I was holding for him. I felt important, like I was a part of the team. I watched the scrimmage intensely, and in that moment, I knew, some day, I would be a football player.

My family ended up moving to another home in Northwest D.C. This time, our house was in the Woodrow Wilson High School neighborhood. I attended Janney Elementary School, a public school that was a mile from my house. I started the fourth grade at the age of nine. I never liked any class work. My report cards all noted I would not apply myself. My favorite subject was recess. There were no actual sports, just games such as kickball and dodgeball. The boys and girls were divided into teams. In the fifth grade, I was the shortest boy, and experienced my first fistfight. We were playing dodgeball, a game where you try to hit a player on the other team with a rubber ball that is approximately the same size as a volleyball. I had a good arm, and struck a boy on the opposing team with the ball. He called me a "dirty Jew." I went after him, hitting him several times with my fists. When he went down, I continued to punch him until a teacher pulled me off him. My only thought at that time was that the school would tell my mom and she would give me a beating. However, another boy playing the game with us told the teacher what the boy had called me. The teacher saved me by never reporting the incident to my mom. After that fight, I knew I could take care of myself.

I did many stupid things in elementary school in order to get attention from other students. There was a Sears and Roebuck store across the street from Janney School. We were not allowed to leave the school grounds during school hours. I sneaked off the grounds during lunch period and went into Sears and stole some candy, but I got caught. My mom had to come to the school to hear from the principal that I was to be kicked out of school. She asked, "Where will he go?" The principal suggested the Catholic School, Saint Ann's, which was next to the grounds of our school. My mom pleaded with him to let me back in Janney, and he did let me back.

I took a whipping that I thought I would never forget; but I did.

The next year, I was in sixth grade, and at lunchtime, again, I sneaked off the school grounds to buy myself an ice cream cone at

High's Ice Cream Store, which was across a busy thoroughfare in front of the school. I went behind the store, so as not to be seen eating it.

By the time I finished the cone, I realized I was going to be late for my one o'clock class. I took off running on the gravel lot behind the store. I slid on the gravel, onto a rusted car fender that was lying on the ground. I could not move. My lower leg was slashed open and still on the edge of the rusted fender. A woman on her apartment porch above the back side of High's started screaming when she saw me kneeling in the puddle of blood. A man in a car on an adjacent street heard the woman screaming, and drove onto the gravel lot. He came over to where I was kneeling, picked me up, with blood all over me, and set me in his car. He took me across town to the emergency room of the hospital.

I never knew or found out who the woman and man were who saved my life.

At the hospital, they immediately gave me transfusions. I had lost a lot of blood. Then, they cleaned the wound of the rust from the fender. My lower leg was sewn up inside and out with over two hundred stitches. The hospital staff contacted my mom. We didn't have a car, so she took a cab across town to the hospital. The doctors told my mom that I might never walk again.

I stayed in the hospital almost a week and eventually went home. I missed the rest of the school year, which was approximately three months. I used crutches for a long time in order to get around. I remember summertime and sitting on the front porch, watching all my friends playing games on the street in front of my house. During the summer after the accident, I learned to walk and run again. I repeated the sixth grade in order to graduate from Janney Elementary School.

I honestly believe this event in the early years of my life had to be God's work. He saved my life and also had me walk and run again in order for me to accomplish something and to be an influence to others who were involved with me later in my life.

BOYS CLUB AND JUNIOR HIGH SCHOOL

The most changing moment of my life was when I traveled nearly ten miles south of D.C. by streetcar to play organized sports at the Georgetown Boys Club. I was twelve years old when I first went there. It was located behind a filling station in a very small abandoned church that was made into a gym, where we dressed and also played basketball. There were about thirty yards of a grass field next to the building where we practiced football. I was an outsider in the Georgetown neighborhood and in the Boys Club, and I was given a tough time by one of the tough guys at the Club. I asked him if he was so tough without all of his friends around him and challenged him to go down the hill next to the practice field in the park with just me to see how tough he really was by himself. We had a brief fistfight and he conceded. After that, I was respected. He and I ended up becoming best friends.

The Georgetown neighborhood at that time was the toughest neighborhood in D.C. There were a bunch of run down, connected town houses and many cobblestone streets with streetcar tracks running down the main thoroughfare. The town was well over a hundred years old, and it showed. Many years later, it was refurbished. It became the place to live. The homes were completely renovated. It became a prestigious, affluent neighborhood.

At the Georgetown Boys Club, my most influential mentor was my first coach, Joe Branzell. He introduced me to football, basketball, and baseball. He treated all of us boys as adults. He demanded discipline and taught us the price we had to pay to be winners, or rather champions. We won all the time, and we played in the city championships in all sports.

Later on, I had another coach, Sleepy Thompson, who assisted Joe Branzell. He was a coach made from the same mold as Joe.

I played on Georgetown Boys Club's 80 lb. football team and eventually 120 lb. football team. I also played two seasons of basketball and three seasons of baseball. One of the seasons of baseball, our team not only won the 19 and under city championship in D.C., but also went to the 19 and under national championship in Johnstown, PA. We were the runner-up in the nation. I could not go to Johnstown to play the national tournament because my dad had a heart attack in 1953, and I had to stay close to home and work construction in nearby Virginia to help support the family.

We played football and baseball games on Saturdays on the Ellipse. This was a large field that was between the White House and the Washington Monument. Two or three games could be played simultaneously because the field was such a big area. Several times, President Truman would take a Saturday walk from the White House to come shake hands with some of the young players. He had secret service men walking along side him with machine guns in golf bags worn over their shoulders.

In 1948, I started junior high school at Alice Deal in D.C. I was thirteen and starting seventh grade, after repeating the sixth grade. There were not any organized team sports, except basketball, which was played against other inner city junior high school teams. I continued to play football and baseball at Georgetown Boys Club. In the ninth grade at Alice Deal, I played basketball and became the top scorer and captain. There were no tournaments to name city champions.

While I was playing basketball in junior high, a situation with my brother Joe came about. He had painted an abstract oil painting on a large piece of plywood, which was kept in the garage. I needed a backboard for a basketball rim that I had. The painting looked like a failure so I sawed the wood to the size of the basketball backboard and attached the rim to it. I then took it two blocks down the street and put it up on a telephone pole in an alleyway so I could practice basketball. The neighbors and I played one-on-one or two-on-two basketball games in that alleyway. Several weeks later Joe went into the garage to retrieve his painting. When I told him what I had done, he knocked the hell out of me, but I got better in basketball because of the many hours practicing in that alleyway.

While in junior high, I had three heroes in the sports world. In football, my hero was Sammy Baugh, the quarterback for the Washington Redskins. In basketball, it was Bob Cousy, Boston Celtics' champion. But the person I looked up to the most was Joe Lewis, the heavyweight-boxing champion of the world. I walked three blocks from our house on a cold, snowy night to watch Joe

Lewis fight for the World Boxing Championship on television. We didn't have a TV in our house at the time, so I went at night to a closed TV store and scratched a circle on a frosted window where they were showing the fight on TV inside the store. I stood outside and watched the entire fight. Joe Lewis won the World Championship, and from that day on, I loved boxing.

HIGH SCHOOL

I entered Woodrow Wilson High School in 1951 at the age of sixteen. During my sophomore year, I played junior varsity football and basketball, and varsity baseball.

The music chapter of my life started when I was in junior high school. Both my older brothers were great musicians. Phil played the piano, and Joe played the drums. Mom thought that I should play an instrument, too. I went to a pawnshop and found a used trumpet. Even though they called it a Cavalier Horn, it was actually a trumpet. Years later, I tried to sell it at the pawnshop, and the man said that it " ... would be better made into a lamp."

Mom got in touch with a man who gave trumpet lessons in a small room in downtown D.C. on Saturdays. I think she got the name from my brother, Joe. The lessons started in the summer of my last year in junior high school. I only went two times. The instructor was either drunk or having a hangover, both sessions, and besides the lessons were interfering with baseball at Georgetown Boys Club; so I quit.

I still had the horn my sophomore year when I went to Wilson High School. I didn't like homeroom. I thought it was a waste of time. The orchestra rehearsed during homeroom, so I joined the orchestra to get out of sitting in homeroom. I could not play a note. The conductor sprang a surprise tryout to see who would be first, second, or third chair. All the instrument sections were trying out. When it came to the trumpet section, and my turn came up, I put my horn down on the chair and walked over to Mr. Essers, a very short-tempered teacher, and whispered in his ear that I didn't know how to play, but I loved music, which I did and do to this day. He was mad and told me to go back to my homeroom.

The next day, Mr. Essers called me out of homeroom and told me he would teach me the trumpet. For about three to four months, I sat alone in the band room during homeroom period, when the orchestra was practicing in the auditorium. He gave me the beginner trumpet book, where I learned to play the scales and to read music. At the end of some of the homeroom periods, he would come in to see how much I had learned reading music and playing the trumpet. I also started practicing at home in the evenings. About half way through the year, he invited me to join the orchestra. I was last chair in the trumpet section, of course.

During my senior year, I became the first chair in the orchestra, and I played several solos during assemblies.

At our 50th reunion of the Class of 1953, some athletes were gathered together in conversation, when a female classmate approached me and said, "I remember you." That got the attention of all the gathered athletes. She said, "You played the trumpet in the orchestra." The guys laughed. She remembered me for the trumpet and not for being the captain of our champion football team, champion basketball team, and runner-up baseball team.

34

My junior year at Woodrow Wilson High, I played fullback in football and guard in basketball. I made the All-High and All-Metropolitan teams. The All-High was in inter-high city League. All-Metropolitan was made up of inter-high City, Catholic League and Northern Virginia League. I also played catcher in baseball and made that all-high team, too. We had great winning seasons in all three sports.

My senior year, we won the inter-high and the Metropolitan championship in football. In the Inter-high school championship, we beat Western High School, and for the Metropolitan High School championship, we beat St. Johns, a private parochial school. The Metropolitan championship game was played in the D.C. professional Washington Redskins football team's stadium, Griffith Stadium. The game was played at night under the lights. After we won the game, a riot broke out, making this game the last high school football championship played at night in D.C.

#33 Lonnie Herzbrun – Wilson High

I made both All-High and All-Metropolitan football. These teams were composed of the high schools' top football athletes in the D.C. and Northern Virginia areas. I was the top scorer in the 1953 football season. I tied this record with a teammate Mike Sommers. We both scored sixty-six points. He would have had more points than I did, but he missed a game against a Northern Virginia team, George Washington, in which we tied 6 to 6 on our way to an undefeated season. That tie made a lasting impression on me the rest of my football career. Although we did not lose the game, after it was over, I didn't feel like celebrating because we hadn't won. The game had been futile.

Another reason Mike did not score more than I scored was that I was the fullback, but I called the plays. When we were near the goal line, I called my own number to carry the ball. I had great confidence in my ability to score. Mike was a great football and track star, who eventually, after college, played professional football. My longest run in my senior year was ninety-four yards against Roosevelt High School, a well-established winning team.

One day during my senior year at Wilson High School, I went across town with a friend "Mole" Jarnigan, who played tailback in football at Wilson a year before I started going to school there. "Mole" was quite the tough little guy and a good boxer in his weight class. He took me to a small gym several miles from our neighborhood. I got in the ring with a guy in my weight class. I held my own, and loved boxing right away. After that day, I would go to the gym by myself on my motorcycle. I trained for several months. I became proficient in rope jumping, which was a tool for conditioning and footwork. Later in life it served me well in dancing. Whether it was the Jitterbug, Foxtrot, or even a Waltz, I performed the steps to the rhythm of the tune playing.

Later on, I boxed a couple of rounds at Hurst Playground. I put the gloves on with a bigger, older guy named Gary Jawish. He was about three years older and thirty-five pounds heavier than I was. Gary fought Cassius Clay (Muhammad Ali) in the Golden Gloves finals in Madison Square Garden in 1960, where he lost by a TKO. Gary knocked the hell out of me, which ended my thoughts of a boxing career.

During my senior year in 1953, our basketball team was Inter-high champion, beating Roosevelt who had a nineteen-game winning streak. I was the top scorer in the Washington Metropolitan area with 199 points averaging twenty-five points a game and had the record for an Inter-high league game with forty-one points beating McKinley Tech, who at that time had a thirty-game winning streak. I also was awarded the player of the year. The forty-one points record was broken by Elgin Baylor, a future Hall of Famer in the pros. The year he broke the score was either 1954 or 1955, when the Inter-high League was first integrated. In 1953, I made All-Inter-high and All-Metropolitan in basketball.

#3 Lonnie Herzbrun – Wilson High

The great Boston Celtics coach, Red Auerbach, approached me after my senior basketball season and invited me to play basketball in a summer league where I would play with college basketball stars up in the Catskill Mountains in New York. The league was called the Borscht League. The teams were set up to play basketball during the day and earn money waiting on tables at a plush restaurant in the evenings.

I was looking forward to competing in this league, instead of working construction, which I had done every summer along with caddying at different country clubs on Sundays, but unfortunately I didn't get to play for the Borscht League. My dad had his first heart attack that summer, and I had to stay around the house; continuing to work construction in nearby Virginia and caddying on Sundays at different country clubs.

****

I bought a used Harley Davidson motorcycle at the beginning of my senior year of high school. I was the first one to have transportation in our family in D.C. I thought I was something special driving a motorcycle. The bike didn't help me get dates. Mothers wouldn't let their daughters ride on a motorcycle. I never dated that much anyway in high school. To have a date, I had to double with some of my friends who had cars.

A pretty girl I met from Maryland High School invited me to her senior prom when I was a junior in high school. I said yes, and I saved up some money from caddying to buy her a corsage and to pay for a cab to pick her up. I borrowed my brother Joe's pinstripe suit with pegged pants. When we arrived at the country club all the guys were wearing tuxedos. I was so embarrassed for her being with me in my brother's suit that I could not even get up to dance all that evening. I never saw her again.

38

Then, the summer before my senior year, I took a ride on my motorcycle over to the Severn River, right near Annapolis, Maryland. I met another very beautiful girl wearing a swimming suit and sitting on the bank of the river. She invited me to swim across the wide Severn River with her. I was a poor swimmer, and I had been a little afraid of the water since my brother Joe threw me in at Glen Echo swimming pool when I was very young. I couldn't swim at all then, and he had to dive in the water to pull me out.

At any rate, the girl was so pretty I accepted her invitation to swim across the river. I had a difficult time keeping up with her. When we made it to the other side, she said, "Let's start back." I thought there was no way I would make it. So I told her, "I would hate to have to save you, let's walk back over the bridge." She said, "It would be no problem," so she started swimming back across the river. I followed because I didn't want a girl to beat me, and halfway back across the river my arms felt like lead from beating the water. I couldn't take another stroke. I convinced her to go on and I got on my back and floated the rest of the way to the bank. After I got back, I was too embarrassed to see her again. In 1956, she won a gold medal in the Olympics. Her name was Shelly Mann.

Later in my senior year of high school, I rode my motorcycle to a drag speedway at Laurel, Maryland raceway. I had been there once before but I didn't race, just watched. I didn't have any mechanical knowledge on how to adjust the motor to make the bike go faster, but the second time I was determined to race. I took my windshield off and locked my front wheel. I lost the race.

On my way back to D.C., I was traveling on a road in Maryland that led straight into Northwest D.C. I was moving too fast, when a big Chrysler with an elderly man driving went straight through a stop sign and stalled in the middle of the road that I was on. I saw the collision coming almost a half block away. I was going too fast to veer, and my front wheel wasn't locked. If I tried putting on the brakes, I knew the bike would try to throw me, so when I saw I was going to hit the car, I stood on top of my brake and clutch (suicide clutch) pedal and tried to dive over the car. I didn't dive high enough to clear my windshield, and when I collided with the car, it folded on impact and flipped me straight upward into the air.

I saw my whole life go by in a split second. I came down on top of the car. I had a small tear in my pants and a scratch on my thigh where the pants were torn. My motorcycle was completely demolished. The elderly man got out of his car and admitted it was his fault in front of the crowd of witnesses, although I had been driving too fast. The man bought me a new pair of pants and a new Harley motorcycle, which I later sold to a friend. The newspaper wrote it up as a miracle and said that my windshield saved me. God has always looked after me.

Lonnie with motorcycle before the accident

Another time God looked after me was when I was thirteen years old in junior high. One hot summer day, Bobby DeVol a friend from the next block over from my house, and I went to a field with a creek running through it. It was near our houses, across a street into Maryland. My mother, on occasion, had told me to stay out of that creek. I disobeyed, and on that hot day we took our shoes off and waded in the creek. I stepped on some broken glass. My big toe was cut badly enough to need stitches, but instead of going to a doctor to get it sewn up because I was scared my mom would discipline me for going in the creek, I went to Bobby's house and his mom cleaned it up and taped it back together. Bobby stayed with me at his house while his mother was doctoring my toe.

Bobby sent his younger brother ahead to start folding the newspapers (we folded newspapers so that we could toss them on front porches of houses from our bikes). The papers were delivered in a small truck and left on a small grassy area in an intersection of three streets. His younger brother was sitting on the stack of papers that he was folding, when a car driven by a drunk man came over the curb, struck him, and killed him instantly. The driver was a friend of the DeVol family. If I hadn't cut my toe and Bobby's mother hadn't doctored it, I would have also been killed because Bobby, his younger brother and I always sat on the papers and folded them before delivering them.

Bobby DeVol and I delivered newspapers together, and had a large inner-city route, which we divided between us. I had a funeral home on my part of the route. One day I went by the funeral home to collect the fees for the paper delivery. I went through the back door as I normally did and went through the embalming room in order to go upstairs to the office. This day there was a body on the embalming table with a sheet over it. No one else was in the room. As I passed the body, suddenly it sprung up from under the sheet. It scared me half to death. I ran out of the building and swore I would not deliver papers there again. I told Bobby he would have to deliver papers thereafter to the funeral home. Bobby's dad was an undertaker. He explained to me this was not unusual. Sometimes gas would accumulate inside the body and that could make it move. To this day, I don't like to see a person dead in an open casket. People at funeral homes comment, "Doesn't he or she look good." I say, "Hell no, he (or she) looks dead." I'd rather remember them when they were alive. Pictures at the funeral home are a much better way to go.

Thinking back on my Boys Club, junior high and high school days, I really spent a lot of time by myself. My brothers were six and ten years older than I, and during this time period they weren't at home. I would go to a nearby field or playground a lot of times to walk our big Doberman. But, I would imagine I was a great basketball or football player without using a ball, going full speed, beating an imaginary opponent, and becoming the hero. These imaginary repetitions were real to me and because of them, when I actually played in a real game; I had a lot of experience, which gave me a great deal of confidence. In boxing, the term used for these exercises was "shadow boxing."

Growing up and all the way through my college days, we never had any dumbbells, barbells, or weightlifting machines. I always worked physically as a construction worker during summer months. While working construction, there were many jobs that required me to carry a "hod," which is a trough carried over the shoulder with a handle similar to a broom handle attached to the bottom to balance the load. I carried bricks or mortar (mud) in the hod.

In high school, since I lived inner-city, all the streets had manhole covers that covered the underground sewers. These sewer covers were approximately 75 to 80 lbs. of iron with two small holes on opposite sides in the top. The holes were there in order to enable the use of a tool to raise the top. I would put two fingers in each hole to raise the cover up enough to place it on the edge of the opening. I would then place my hands on opposite sides of the manhole cover and lift it above my head, doing several repetitions. None of my friends could do that, and I knew I had a gift of strength, which also gave me so much confidence.

3rd QUARTER

COLLEGE

I had many scholarship offers to different universities, in 1953, for both football and basketball, and I had an offer to play baseball in the minor leagues. I really didn't know if I was ready for college. My oldest brother Phil stayed on my back until I said I would accept the scholarship to the University of Tennessee. I chose Tennessee because they had won the National Championship in 1951, and the head coach General Neyland, who was a legend, showed interest in me. He had different assistant coaches call me several times, always saying they wanted me at the University of Tennessee. He also sent two players from the 1951 championship team, Bill Pearman and Ted Daffer, to talk to me in D.C. At that time, I believe, both men were in the Army, and they were stationed near D.C. In 1951, when Tennessee won the National Championship, I was a sophomore in high school. During that season, they had beaten a good local team, Maryland, 28-13.

After committing to go to Tennessee, there was an article in the Washington Newspaper on corrupt cities in the U.S. The third city listed was Knoxville, Tennessee. They said the city was in a dry county with many illegal bootleggers selling whiskey and moonshine which was made in the surrounding mountain areas. The city had many nightclubs with illegal gambling and serving illegal liquor. There were prostitution houses throughout the city. The people committing these illegal actions were paying off the city and county officials. I found after being in the Knoxville area, all of these stories were true. I noticed when we went to downtown Knoxville that all the policemen walking their beats were very old.

When I took the train from D.C., I really didn't know what to expect in Knoxville, Tennessee, 500 miles away. I had to take the train because freshmen football players weren't allowed to have cars, trucks, or motorcycles. It was my first time away from home. I had hardly ever gone outside of the D.C. area. My family never took vacations.

When we football players showed up on the practice field, there were approximately 130 freshmen scholarship players (I think from that 1953 class only thirteen of us graduated). There was no limit on football scholarships. I played fullback at 175 lbs. There were at least twelve freshmen fullbacks when they lined up for sprints. After the second week, because of the severity of two-a-day practices, conditioning, and scrimmaging, over forty freshmen players left to go back home or went somewhere else to play. Also, up until the day classes started, one or two freshmen players would leave every day.

The football gear was not that good. The practice pants were canvas, the shirts were wool, which got very hot, and the helmets were a plastic outer shell with webbing inside that was held with rivets that cut your forehead when you hit someone. There were no facemasks or mouthpieces, and we wore high top shoes. In two-a-day practices, we wore the same jock and socks, wet and sweaty, during the morning session and again in the afternoon practice. They gave us cornstarch to put on the groin areas so we wouldn't get jock itch; we also put it in between our toes not to get a fungus known as athlete's foot. We also wore the same shirt and pants. Nothing dried from morning practice to the afternoon practice.

We never had water during practice. After practice, they supplied salt water, which tasted terrible. We then had to run next to train tracks back to the stadium, a quarter of a mile, where there were showers and dressing rooms. Almost every practice, the players would lose 10 to 12 pounds of water weight. The athletics' dorm was three floors in the East Stadium, and there was no air conditioning or fans in the rooms. The training table where we ate meals was also in the East Stadium.

My scholarship consisted of tuition, books, three meals a day, housing, and fifteen dollars a month, which we used for incidentals. This money, in most cases, didn't last two weeks. The money was really supposed to be for laundry. To save money, we snuck into the laundry room under the East Stadium, where they washed and dried our practice uniforms in huge commercial washers and dryers. Late at night, several of us washed and dried our personal stuff in those washers and dryers. They knew we were sneaking in the laundry room, but they never knew how we got in, because the doors were always locked. The hinges were on the outside of the doors, so we took a hammer and a screwdriver and knocked the pins out of the hinges, opened the door, then replaced them.

The East Stadium, where I lived, also had a lounge area with a ping-pong table, several couches, and one TV. When I first went in to watch TV, there was a guy on the screen imitating a hillbilly. I thought he was a comedian. Later, I found out that was the way he really spoke. It was Cas Walker, a wealthy grocery man; he was on all three television stations every day of the week at 6:00 p.m. I had never heard anyone speak like he did.

Freshmen were not eligible for varsity play, and practically our whole purpose as freshmen football players was to be the scout team versus the varsity, which meant we scrimmaged against them using the next opponent's offense and defense. We, the freshman, ran the "T" formation plays of the varsity's next opponent. Tennessee was the only team among major colleges using the single wing at that time. In fact, it was the only team running the single wing my senior year, 1957. The quarterback was Johnny Majors and I was the fullback.

During our freshmen year, we did play five freshmen games without using Tennessee's single wing. We only practiced "T" formation against varsity, so we used some of those plays. One game was against Kentucky, and we traveled by bus. I sat next to Johnny Majors, from Huntland, Tennessee. I wanted to be accepted by the Tennessee guys, so I struck up a conversation with Johnny. I was looking out the window of the fast moving bus when I saw a barn, and commented, "Look at all those foxes hanging in that barn." Johnny laughed out loud because it was tobacco, which I had never seen, nor had I ever seen a fox either. The bus was going so fast that that's what it appeared to be. Remember, I was an inner-city boy who didn't get very far outside the city and didn't know the real countryside.

Another story of how naïve I was of the countryside happened years later while attending the University. I was courting my wife, Wilma. We were walking through the countryside when I saw an animal and said to her, "That's the largest sewer rat I have ever seen!" She laughed because it was an opossum. Again, growing up I hadn't gotten outside the concrete of the big city.

My sophomore season was in 1954. General Neyland had retired after the 1953 season and Harvey Robinson, who was on General Neyland's staff, took his place as head coach. Harvey Robinson and his staff only lasted one season. They were fired after winning 4 games and losing 6.

A week before the 1954 season started, I broke a rib in a scrimmage. Our trainer, Mickey O'Brian, said I only had a contusion. I couldn't breathe without a great deal of pain. I even moved my mattress to the floor, so it wouldn't bend as much, which slowed down the pain. I still went to practices, but I couldn't do contact work. My ribs were still causing me pain, so one day, on my own, I went to the infirmary on campus. They x-rayed my ribs and found out one was broken. I took the x-ray back to Mickey O'Brian, and he gave me hell for going on my own to the infirmary.

I was what they called 'red shirted' in the 1954 season. That gave me an extra year of scholarship in football and education. It was during that time that I started to pay more attention to academics.

The 1955 season was now my sophomore year, and that was when the great Coach Bowden Wyatt and his staff were hired from Arkansas. In the 1954 Arkansas season, they played in the Cotton Bowl on New Year's Day in 1955. Coach Wyatt was also an All-American and he played on General Neyland's 1938 team that was the National Football Champion.

Coach Wyatt got everybody's attention in a scrimmage the first day of training when Tom Tracy, the top running back in the SEC and the best athlete I ever saw, then or now, went down with leg cramps. Coach Wyatt moved the team up, leaving Tom on the ground, and continued the scrimmage. Coach knew Tom's history: he was never disciplined; he had leg cramps because he broke all training rules; and he had to be forced to go to classes. The trainers came and got Tom up and over to the sidelines, and Coach Wyatt told an assistant coach after practice to tell Tom to pack his bags and that he was through. Tom went up to Canada to play pro-football and later on had a career with the Detroit Lions in the NFL.

I witnessed some of Tom's unbelievable physical abilities. In 1954, we went to a public swimming pool in Concord. We went there all the time but I had never seen Tom there. We had an end on the football team named Ron Gust, who in his home state was a champion diver. When he would perform on the high board everyone got out of the pool and watched. That day, Tom showed up in a borrowed swimsuit. He had very muscular legs and was only about 5'8". He looked like he had never been in the sun because he was very pale. When Ron got through with his diving exhibition, Tom got on the high dive and outperformed Ron on different dives. You could have heard a pin drop from the people watching from outside of the pool. They stood there in awe of his performance.

Another time in 1954 in our lounge in the East Stadium, a professional ping-pong player, an oriental man, came to entertain the players on the football team. All of us who played ping-pong in the lounge took turns playing the ping-pong pro. There were about five of us taking turns, and the most points any of us could get were about three. Tom came in late watching us play. Finally, when all of us were through, Tom came up to the table and motioned with a paddle that he wanted to take on the pro. I had never seen him playing ping-pong in the lounge. The first game he scored eight points. It was time for bed check, but everyone stayed in the lounge to watch Tom play the pro in another game, in which he beat the pro.

Before I broke my rib in 1954, a drill was set up for the fullbacks to learn to dive over the goal line when we were close to it. They set up dummies on top of one another, five-feet high, so the fullbacks could practice diving over them with the ball in our hands. All the fullbacks were hitting the dummies with their chests, barely making it over, but when it was Tom's turn, he did a full flip, landing on his feet. The coach told him to go on in. The rest of us stayed and struggled through the drill.

That spring football practice before the upcoming 1955 season, I had to have two operations on my nose in order to remove some cartilage and bones so I could breathe better. When we were in the huddle, no one could hear the plays called because of my loud breathing. Coach Bowden Wyatt said, "Get the sick horse out of the huddle."

In the 1955 season opening game against Mississippi State, which we lost 13-7, I started at offensive fullback and defensive halfback. I was the leading ground gainer for that game, but I fumbled twice. I had broken two fingers catching baseballs my senior year in high school, and instead of setting them, they pulled the fingers out and taped them to a finger next to them, and I continued to play with the broken fingers. This caused me to have no strength in my right hand fingers, so I was susceptible to fumbling. One of General Neyland's axioms is still put on a black board before each game: *the team that made the fewest mistakes, wins.* Fumbling the ball was a definite mistake.

The rest of the season, I played second string and a great fullback, Tommy Bronson, started. I did end that season leading the team with three interceptions on defense. I kidded with Johnny Majors my junior year that they actually moved me to play

53

offensive guard because I outgained him in the Mississippi game in 1955.

The 1955 season, we won six games, lost three and tied one. The Gator Bowl invited us to play Auburn. Coach Wyatt turned it down because in the next season, 1956, our first opponent was Auburn, and Coach Bowdon did not want them to see the Tennessee single wing.

The 1956 season was a great season with ten wins and one loss. The loss was in the Gator Bowl, which was played after the regular season, and it didn't count in the standings. We won the SEC and were second in the nation to Oklahoma, who was number one.

Johnny Majors, Tennessee tailback, was ranked for the Heisman trophy, which became a political award. Here is how the balloting turned out for the Heisman trophy: No. 1, Paul Horning from Notre Dame. His team record was 2 wins and 8 losses, and he was the quarterback on a losing team. No. 2, Johnny Majors from Tennessee. He was the tailback (quarterback). The record for our number two team in the nation and in the regular season was 10 wins and 0 losses (bowl games didn't count at that time). No. 3, Tommy MacDonald from the number one team in the nation, Oklahoma. No. 4, another Oklahoma player, Jerry Tubbs, a lineman. No. 5, argumentatively the greatest running back of all times, Jim Brown, from Syracuse.

The Sugar Bowl game, New Year's Day 1957, closing out the 1956 season, was between Tennessee and Baylor. We lost 13 to 7. I've always thought this game was lost because of an incident that happened in the game. We had a great guard, Bruce Burnham, and he was on his knees at the end of a play, when a player from Baylor kicked him under the chin (like his head was a football). He went into convulsions and did not regain consciousness when they carried him off the field to the hospital. The Baylor player was kicked out of the game, but the damage had already been done. All the Tennessee players' thoughts for the remainder of the game would be whether Bruce would make it or not. He survived with no after effects, thank God.

In 1956, the rule at Tennessee was that you couldn't get married and remain on scholarship. Eventually the rule did change. I got engaged to Wilma Brown, a pretty, intelligent, and sensitive girl. That combination makes a girl beautiful. My thought, through my whole life, was that I never had any regards for an ugly girl. I married Wilma on June 1, 1957.

During the spring football practice for the upcoming season's 1957 team, I beat out a fine football player, Bobby Urbano, for the starting left guard on offense and left defensive tackle positions. After three weeks of spring training, I had to go home to D.C. My father had died. When I came back to get ready for the season, I looked at the team roster and noticed that I was listed as the second team because I missed the last week of spring football practice. I had already won first string. I went over to Coach Hitt, my position coach, and said to him that I wanted to be third string so I could scrimmage against the first team, in order to regain first string status. I did regain first string status before the season started.

Back then a player played both offensive and defensive positions. It turned out in the 1957 season that we only had three guards ready to play, so I played guard and tackle on the left side with the first unit and guard offense and right tackle on defense with the second unit. Coach Hitt stated in the paper that I was the only Tennessee lineman ever to play sixty minutes, the whole game, which I did practically the whole 1957 season. After each game on Saturday it took me until Thursday to regain my full strength in order to play again the next Saturday.

Frank Kolinsky and I were the two heaviest linemen on our team. Frank came back for the 1957 season at 240 lbs. I came back at 220 lbs. They put both of us on the fat man's table (That meant for lunch during two-a-day practices prior to the season, we had only a wedge of lettuce). We both ended up weighing 205 lbs. when the season started.

During the 1957 season, we were playing Maryland. The university was in College Park, close to my home in D.C. My brother, Phil, took my mom, who had never seen me play sports, not even in high school, to see me play.

After the game, Phil asked my mom what she had thought of my play. She said, "If he thinks he's bringing that uniform home for me to wash, he has another thought coming to him." She had worried the whole game about having to wash my uniforms.

The coaches awarded me the game ball after the game mainly because I was from nearby D.C. I didn't have a great game, but I did recover two fumbles. The balls rolled under me. When the coaches awarded me the game ball in front of the team, I said, "Thanks, this is the first time I've seen it all day." We beat Maryland that day, 13 to 0.

We had a good 1957 season by winning eight games and losing three. This included the Gator Bowl, in which we beat Texas A&M, a great team, with the Heisman trophy winner, John David Crow, and legendary coach Bear Bryant.

When we arrived in Jacksonville Florida for the Gator Bowl that season, we had a police escort on motorcycles to a restaurant. Frank Kolinsky and I both loved motorcycles and when the team, coaches, and policemen went inside, Frank and I stayed outside. We noticed that one of the motorcycles had the keys still in the ignition. We thought we would take a little ride around the block on the cop's motorcycle. The streets were all one way, and we got lost in Jacksonville. We didn't even know the name of the restaurant.

When we finally found our way back to the group, everyone was finished eating and was outside in the parking lot, including the coaches and the policeman who had driven the motorcycle. We parked the bike and got quietly onto the bus thinking Coach Wyatt would surely send us back to Knoxville.

We were holding our breath the whole time we were in Jacksonville practicing for the game. Coach didn't send us back, however, but we both knew we had better have a great game. I believe the competitive spirit sometimes makes you do stupid, daring things with no regard to consequences.

Lonnie at University of Tennessee

During that game, there was a great collision between our fine tailback and defensive safety, Bobby Gordon, and their All-American halfback, John David Crow. Both players were knocked out and finally Bobby got up, groggy, but they carried Crow to the sideline where he stayed out of the game for a long period of time. We won the game with a field goal, 3 to 0.

The rule in college football at that time, in 1957, was that you couldn't play after graduating even if you were working toward a Master's Degree. I had enough hours to graduate in four years because I was red shirted. I held back one subject my fourth year working towards my Bachelor's Degree. This way I could play my fifth year while also working on my Master's Degree. I ended up going up on the stage three times when I graduated in 1958. I received my Bachelor's Degree in Education, my Master's Degree in Supervision and Administration, and my Regular Army Commission, Second Lieutenant.

****

After my graduation, I took my wife and another couple, who were our good friends from Tennessee, to my hometown, Washington D.C. During our visit I took them to meet my aunt and uncle in their haberdasher store in downtown. The store was packed with customers, and when I entered the store my aunt hollered, from the back of the store, "Is that you, Lonnie?"

I said, excitedly, "Yes!"

She said, "You used to be such a nice looking boy."

Everyone turned and looked at me. My friends had a good laugh. Not wearing a facemask in football takes its toll.

****

Much later, after college, I visited the Holocaust museum in D.C. with two of my teammates, Frank Kolinsky and Mike LaSorsa. Going through the museum reminded me of an incident when I was a small boy in Washington, D.C. A Rabbi from Ohio visited us at our home. He looked up the Herzbrun name, which was also his name, in a telephone directory. He still had numbers tattooed on his wrist that were put there when he was imprisoned in the German Concentration camp, Auschwitz, Poland. This camp put 20,000 Jews a day to death; Hitler's *Final Solution* for completely eliminating the Jews. This rabbi had survived because the war ended against the Germans. He told us, "There were over 500 Herzbruns from Hungary put in the ovens (cremated) at Auschwitz."

As I started walking through the museum with my friends, I could only go part of the way. I became emotionally sick and had to leave. An ironic thought came to my mind – God had created man because he was disappointed with the monkey. I thought: what would God create next, after seeing the results of mankind in the past many centuries?

U.S. ARMY AND PRO-FOOTBALL

I received an invitation my senior year into the Scabbard and Blade, an honorary fraternity.

I graduated from the University of Tennessee in 1958 with a Regular Army Commission rather than a Reserve Commission; a great honor given only to those with high academic and ROTC standing.

I took the Regular Army Commission because, at that time, I planned to make a career of the Army. After graduation, my orders were to report to Fort Benning, Georgia to Infantry Officers Basic Course. I graduated in 1958 from that course and went directly into the Airborne Course (Paratrooping).

After graduation, I went into the Ranger Training Course; this later became the Green Beret Unit. This course was the most physical course the Army had to offer.

The first week of Ranger Training was at Fort Benning, Georgia. It consisted of conditioning, hand-to-hand combat, and fundamentals of patrolling. The second week was patrolling in

Florida. When we arrived in camp, the first thing they had us do was walk into the swamp, which was pitch black water infested with alligators all around us. I never knew they wouldn't attack unless you irritated them.

I had a problem after several days of patrolling with very little sleep. We came off a patrol early in the morning, and were cleaning our rifles when a guy next to me knocked his bayonet off the table. It stuck through my boot into the top of my foot. I continued to patrol, but my foot become infected and swelled up, so I could barely tie up my boot. They wanted me to start the course over at a later date. I wasn't going to repeat two weeks of hell. I told them, "Hell no, I am going on." They shot me with antibiotics, and I continued the swamp phase of the course.

All through the course, they would test your courage. They put a log across the river with a rope tied under it. The log was about fifteen-feet above the river. You had to shimmy up the rope to get on top of the log and then balance while walking on top of the log to the other side of the swamp, with demolition going off underneath. Then, you had to reach the rope underneath, and, while hanging, using hand over hand movement, you had to reach the middle of the swamp. Then you asked permission for Ranger Herzbrun to drop. You landed in the swamp water and swam around a huge alligator, nose to nose. After everyone went through the test, they treated us with a meal consisting of alligator meat, which they cooked on an open pit. It tasted like steak, but it was too tough to swallow.

All patrols took place at night. We had schooling in the daytime, and patrolling started in the late evenings and continued through the night. There were about eight rangers in a patrol, and you followed the rangers in front of you in a line. The point ranger was the only one with the compass. Everyone rotated, during the patrol, to be point man. The ranger last in line, in the light of the evening, always walked backward with his bayonet fixed ... because of the alligators following us through the swamp. When it got dark you turned around because you couldn't see the alligator anyhow. It was so dark you couldn't see the ranger in front of you. You could only see the luminous tape on his hat.

While going on one patrol, a ranger fell asleep walking and stepped in a deeper part of the swamp and his face went underwater.

He then woke up and said aloud, "We're lost." Then he realized that there was no one in front of him. The leaders had never realized that there was no one following behind them. They kept on walking. They had the compass.

The lost rangers gathered together in a circle, sleeping in until daylight. We saw inquisitive alligators surrounding us when the group woke up. Eventually a helicopter arrived to guide us out of the swamp. By the next patrol we found out how to get a little sleep. The next patrol we designated who would fall asleep.

The next phase was patrolling in the mountains of Georgia. Our last patrol in the mountain phase was hiking twenty-five miles to reach a dam, simulating blowing it up, and returning twenty-five miles to base camp. I was carrying a large weapon, a Browning automatic rifle. They put me with a small guy from New York City, and I was from D.C. Neither one of us had hunted before. We had to find our own food and water during this two-day patrol. We were getting hungry and thirsty.

We got our water by filling our canteens up from a little stream. For food, I found a box turtle. I said to my partner, "I've always heard that turtle soup was good to eat." I killed it, took his insides out of the shell, put it in my canteen cup, and added water. I cooked it over a small fire. I took a bite, but it was so bitter that I spit it out. My partner tried, he did the same. I found out later that a salt-water turtle was good to eat, not a box turtle. We found a green apple tree and filled our shirts with apples and ate them for the two-day patrol.

Again during this phase, they set up another test of courage. The test was called "Death Slide." You climb up a tree 30 feet high, limb by limb, until you reach a small platform attached to the tree where a cadre waited to hand you a small hook. There was a cable hooked to a taller tree behind the platform that we were standing on. This cable went down and across a river and was tied to another tree, on the other bank of the river. The hook you placed over the cable was only big enough for two fingers of the right hand and two fingers from the left hand on top of the two right fingers. You flew down the cable hollering, "Ranger." You couldn't let go until another cadre, on the far bank, waved a white flag. Being as heavy as I was, I came down faster than most, and when I hit the water, it knocked me out. They pulled me out of the water to the bank.

This whole course was tough. It was designed to teach us to function under stress. I thought it taught me to be miserable. I already knew how to be miserable, so my thought was, "Why?"

For my next assignment, I got orders to report to Fort Campbell, Kentucky with the 101st Airborne Group, a strategic air command unit. I was with the 321st Battle Group. General Westmoreland who later commanded the Vietnam War commanded the 101st. When I arrived at Fort Campbell, he personally asked if I would play football for the 101st division. He was a general you could not turn down.

I became captain of the 1959 and 1960 football teams, and both were the Army champions. I made All-Army both years while at Fort Campbell. I went to Jump Master School, and ended up with thirty jumps.

When I first got to Fort Campbell, five paratroopers were dragged to death when a sudden, big wind came up on the drop zone. They couldn't get to their feet in order to run around and collapse their chutes, which caught the extreme ground wind. After that tragedy, the airborne put a quick release latch on the harness. If you couldn't get to your feet, the chute was released so you would not be dragged over the landing zone.

Also at Fort Campbell, I received an accommodation from General Westmoreland for implementing a conditioning / weight program for my Battle Group, which later was adapted for the whole 101st division. We did a mass jump, which is a whole division of paratroopers jumping from many airplanes at different levels in the sky. It gets very crowded in the air with paratroopers.

Sometimes a paratrooper would end up walking on top of a fellow paratrooper's chute. The lower paratrooper's chute would steal the air of the paratrooper's chute above him and collapse it. He would then have to climb down the risers of the lower paratrooper, both coming down together holding on to each other. This was not a good situation, as now I was weighing 230 pounds. I came down fast enough without another person accompanying me on the same chute.

During one mass jump, General Westmoreland was jumping with the division and he asked me, in the plane, if I wanted to jump wind dummy with him. Of course I said, "Yes, sir." That means the first time the plane makes a pass over the drop zone, we would be the only ones jumping, to test the wind. We were jumping from

64

a 130 Transport plane. The door was open with General Westmoreland standing in the door, trying to smoke a cigarette, with 100 mph wind going by the open door from the propellers. I said, "General, the green light is on," and he walked out of door but nothing happened to him. The wind knew who it was dealing with ... the general!

I jumped far out of the plane, so I wouldn't be blown against the fuselage. I didn't want to hit the ground unconscious.

My next assignment was in Fort Eustis, Virginia, where I would be attending transportation school in order to later become a helicopter pilot. I had previously taken flying lessons through the Reserve Officers Training Corps. at the University of Tennessee. I had received my Single-Engine Pilot's License then, but I hadn't flown since.

It was during my flying lessons in Tennessee, as I was taking my first solo cross-country flight, with nineteen hours of flight time under my belt, that I experienced my most dramatic incident in the air.

I took off from Knoxville airport, going first to a small airfield in Gadsden, Alabama, then on to Birmingham. I started back the same day. The sky was getting very dark, although it was still early afternoon. At that time, I didn't know how to call the tower in Gadsden, so I landed the plane there and walked up to the tower to find out how the weather was going into Knoxville. The tower controller said, "It will be okay." So, I took off from Gadsden and flew over the mountains.

As I flew over the mountains, I got in the worst storm there could ever be. The wind caused so much turbulence that it turned the light plane upside down. When I took the steering stick to the opposite direction to upright the plane, it happened again and again.

It seemed to me I was bouncing upside down and back, over and over.

I was in the cockpit of the light cub cruiser, a plane in which the gas gauges were outside hanging under the wing. The weather outside was so bad that I couldn't see the gauges. I was so scared. I was soaking wet from fear, and I felt like I was going to die. I didn't have any control of the plane. As a last resort, I decided to give it my best try. I started to fly the plane away from the mountains. I didn't know exactly where I was. I eventually saw the Tennessee River.

I dropped the plane down low and when I saw lights of cars. I thought, but couldn't really tell, that they were on Highway 411. I followed the lights, but I couldn't actually see the highway. I began to be afraid, because if I didn't see the lights at the airport or Knoxville soon it would mean that I may have veered off slightly, and I would go over Oak Ridge ... which was restricted. I was afraid they would shoot me down.

I missed the airport, but I did finally see the lights from Knoxville, and I was able to turn back without violating the Oak Ridge air space.

I called the tower to get landing instructions. The air controller advised me that the airport was closed. I said, "I have to land. I've been flying around a long while and I can't see my gas gauge. It is out on my wings."

The air controller said, "The wind is so bad, you will have to make a right wheel landing."

I said, "I have never made a wheel landing, only a stalled landing."

They said for me to wait a minute, my instructor was in the vicinity of the tower. In the meantime, I was flying around the airport. My instructor got on the radio and said, "Forget about making a right wheel landing, but you have to make a wheel landing. The wind is up too high." He told me to come in at eighty-five miles per hour instead of sixty-five. I tried landing, but the wind was making it hard to keep the plane in the center of the runway. When the tires hit the runway, I bounced back into the air. I put the stick forward but kept flying.

The instructor said to me, "This next time when your wheels hit and you bounce, leave the stick forward, and we will get you."

I circled the airport again to land, and in the meantime they brought the fire engines out on either side of the runway. Hell, I thought I might hit one of the engines while I was trying to keep the plane, which was swaying from side to side, on the runway. The tires hit the runway and I bounced in the air again, but this time I left the stick forward, and the plane landed. I cut the ignition off while on the runway. I didn't taxi the plane at all. I just got out and took off running toward the tower. By the time I got there, my instructor came down to greet me.

I said, "You can take this flying, and stick it up your ass."

My instructor asked what happened, and I told him about the air controller in Gadsden who had told me the weather in Knoxville was okay.

I left, and the next week my instructor got a hold of me and said, "They fired that air controller in Gadsden." I believe this was just to appease me. I did finish my flying in order to get my single-engine pilot's license. Now you understand why I haven't flown since. I thought I had a better chance of staying alive jumping from planes rather than flying them. This was another time when God looked after me.

****

After graduation from transportation school, I was presented with my First Lieutenant bars. I was asked by General Besson to play football for the Fort Eustis Wheels.

During the season playing for Fort Eustis, in Virginia, we played the most controversial game I have ever heard of; it was against the Quantico Marines. Service football is played under college rules and the officials of the game were high school officials. During the game, we blocked two punts and ran them both back for touchdowns. The referee called both of them back, which is a high school rule, but in college rules, they would have been counted as touchdowns. At the end of the game, we had lost by one touchdown.

The referee was shown the rulebook in college football, and after the game, he reversed the outcome, which gave us the win. That made us East Coast champions. They called General Neyland, who was head of the rules committee, and stated from the college rulebook that the referee is the sole judge of the outcome of the game.

****

We had the opportunity to play the Quantico Marines again in a nationally televised game for the Armed Forces championship, called the Missile Bowl played in Orlando, Florida. We won on a last minute field goal, 25 to 24.

I was captain of the team and was named the most valuable player, All-Army, East Coast Player of the Year, and received the Timmy Award for the outstanding Armed Forces Player of the Year, presented by the Washington Touchdown Club of D.C.

Timmy Award – Armed Forces Player of the Year 1961

The banquet was at the Sheraton Park Hotel in D.C. with over 1500 fans there.

Some of the notables at the banquet were:

- Vice President - Lyndon Johnson, who was a presenter
- Coach of the Year in the Pros - Vince Lombardi, Green Bay Packers
- Player of the Year in the Pros - Paul Hornung, Green Bay Packers
- Coach of the Year, College – Paul Bear Bryant, Alabama
- Player of the Year, College - Ernie Davis, Syracuse
- Special Award in Baseball – Stan Musial, St. Louis

General Besson presenting Lonnie with Bowl Watch

I decided after the football season at Fort Eustis that I wanted to get out of the service. Four reserve officers on our championship team and I had come to our time to get discharged. No one could leave, though, because of the Cuban Missile Crisis. So I asked General Besson, who knew we were getting out, if instead of going back to our units after the football season, could the five of us stay and administer a new physical fitness test, which the Army was begun to require each post to administer to their troops. General Besson agreed, and we were assigned to test all soldiers at Fort Eustis and Fort Story on the beach near Virginia Beach.

I dressed all of our cadre in African helmets, shorts and combat boots. I told them we had to look sharp and professional giving the test or we would have to go back to soldiering with our units.

The Army held our discharge papers up for two more months because of the Cuban Crisis. This whole time we were testing the troops. Also after the season was over, General Westmoreland, who had become the Commandant of West Point, called General Besson asking me to be assigned to West Point in an over strength assignment in transportation, a two-year tour. He wanted me to help coach football at West Point.

General Westmoreland flew me up to West Point and had a colonel escort me around the building, stadium, and grounds. I didn't have the courage to tell him that I had decided I was going to get out of the army to play professional football. So when I got back, I asked General Besson to call and tell him for me.

I considered it a great honor for him to ask me to help coach at West Point. I would have been coaching with a great coach, Paul Dietzel, who had been hired to be the head coach there. He hadn't

71

reported to West Point when I took the tour of the Academy, but they told me when I visited that he would be coming there.

I was then invited to play in the U.S. Bowl (this is a game played by the NFL draft choices and players selected as free agents). I was a free agent playing on the west side, because I was headed for The Baltimore Colts. After the game, the Washington Redskins, from my hometown, made a push to sign me. I decided to sign with them when the season ended at Fort Eustis. I thought I needed to put on more weight to play in the NFL.

I already weighed 230 pounds when I started lifting weights for the first time in my life. In about eight months, I got my decline bench press up to 505 lbs. This was more impressive because I had long arms, a 37-inch sleeve length. I always felt I had natural strength, and also growing up I had heavy lifting construction jobs. My body weight went up to 255 lbs. Weighing that much was a mistake. I didn't lose speed, but I did lose quickness, and in the pre-season exhibition games, because of my extra weight, I developed shin splints, which hurt my play.

I started a game as a linebacker against the Los Angeles Rams. I had a good game. This game was played at the end of our pre-season camp in Los Angeles. We had four more exhibition games left. While in Los Angeles, they listed on the programs the weights of all the players of the Redskins and the Rams; the heavier players' weights were listed lighter, and the lighter players' weights were listed heavier. I believe to this day this is still happening. When we were playing, I was listed at 230 lbs., but the heavier linemen on the Redskins and the Rams were all listed less than 300 lbs. The scales at the time just went up to 300 lbs., so both teams took their lineman down to the stockyard and marched them individually onto the platform, which existed to weigh cattle.

The Redskins had three players over 300 lbs., and the Rams had twelve over 300 lbs.

I did beat out the middle linebacker from the previous Redskin season, so I brought my family to Washington D.C. the last week before the last exhibition game. They moved me to offensive guard, with no reason; I hadn't played guard in five years. During practice, I missed my block on a starting defensive tackle; he outweighed me by forty pounds. I grabbed him and held onto him. We got into a fight, and I knew if he got on top I wouldn't have a prayer. Thankfully, it was broken up before any damage was really done.

In the fifth and last exhibition game, I played offensive guard, and they moved an offensive tight end to middle linebacker, which was my position. It didn't make any sense. I was released, and the Redskins had already traded New York for their All-Pro middle linebacker, Sam Huff. He was too old to perform as he had with the New York Giants. The Redskins brought him in for gate receipts, because of his name. I then left the Redskins and returned with my family to Tennessee.

****

I didn't have a job. I met with a wrestling promoter, John Cazana, through a mutual friend. John wanted to train me as a professional wrestler. We worked out at the Y.M.C.A. in Knoxville. The villains made the most money in the exhibitions. I didn't want anyone to know who I was so I was going to wear a mask and planned to be called, "The Headsman." This never took place because I couldn't be a good enough actor to fake some of the techniques used in the bouts.

****

My wife Wilma and I were reading the paper and saw an article mentioning that I was the new head coach at Fulton High School. I had never even applied for the job. I didn't even know who to contact to see if this were true. So, I went over to the school, Fulton, to check it out. They informed me I was the new head coach.

I then went and talked to the assistant coaches who were still at Fulton and found out they had applied for the head-coaching job there. They were both disappointed about not getting the job and were going to leave. I said, "If one of you wants to be head coach next season, I'll be an assistant, and we will switch every year, but let's try to make Fulton football team a winner." They stayed, but in the next season neither one of them wanted the head coach position.

Both of these coaches, Buddy Beam and Jerry Scott, were great coaches. We had two other great coaches, Bob Black and Mike LaSorsa, who joined the staff at later dates. We won several city championships and went to five bowl games in the eight-year period. Bob Fry, one of the greatest head basketball coaches in Tennessee, coached the junior varsity football team. The other junior varsity coach was Dickie Sharp, a very successful head track coach.

I later found out how I got the job at Fulton. A player I had played football with at the University of Tennessee, Bo Shafer, found out that I was back in town. His father was on the school board, which selected the head coach for Fulton High School.

4th QUARTER

High School Coaching

I began coaching football at Fulton High School in Knoxville, Tennessee in 1963. We ended the season with three wins, six losses, and one tie. This was the best season Fulton had compared to the two prior seasons. I started coaching before classes began and three weeks before the first game. I met with coaches Buddy Beam, who coached linemen, and Jerry Scott, who coached backs. These two coaches held spring football prior to this season. We had to use the same offensive and defensive systems practiced in the spring because there were only three weeks until the season started. We cut plays out from the offense and defense, to keep them to a minimum in order to get proficient in those plays and to allow the player to gain confidence through repetition.

Our whole practices were geared toward changing their attitudes to paying the price to be a winner. We did this basically with three things.

One was conditioning, because we didn't have enough good players and the ones we had would have to play both offense and

77

defense. Our conditioning methods varied and it separated the players who really wanted to win from the others.

Second was teaching fundamentals, like blocking, tackling, throwing, catching, and running. This was accomplished in small group sessions with full contact and team sessions, whether it would be half line or full team scrimmages.

Third was fixing their attitude. Coaches talked about giving 110%, but most coaches didn't practice it. We did, by teaching full speed, doing your job, and keep going until the whistle is blown.

We emphasized playing each play as if it were the only play of the game. We cut practices down to one hour and a half in order for them to learn to go full speed the whole practice. No loafing or going half speed. This hard type of practice separated the ones who really wanted it by learning the price to pay to be a winner.

At one point, I thought we would have to cancel the season because we ended up with less than thirty players. They had never been pushed so hard.

We had one great player on that team: D.D. Lewis, a senior who played linebacker. He was a tough player who had a great desire to hit someone and to make something happen. D.D. was brought up in a small house in an alley in North Knoxville. He was the youngest of fourteen children. At Fulton, we put him in charge of discipline in the cafeteria where he was fed for performing this job.

D.D. Lewis made All-State and earned a scholarship to Mississippi State where he was All-SEC `66, `67, and SEC defensive player of the year `67, and All-American `67. He was elected to the Knoxville, Tennessee Hall of Famer in 2006. He played professional football for Dallas Cowboys for fourteen years, and played in five Super Bowls and won two Super Bowl Championships.

High school coaching, at Fulton High School, was my first head football coaching job. I was on the stage of the auditorium with the Principal, Dr. James Newman, a very serious, stern looking person. I was called on to talk about our football team.

This was my first time speaking in front of a large audience. During my talk, I had no notes. I was describing our football team, and I blurted out a word used in lingo around players. I said, "We have the hardest 'knockers' in town."

The 1200 students at the assembly roared in laughter. God knows why I used that term. I looked over at Dr. Newman who was looking at me with very stern eyes. I had to hold my composure. I bit the inside of my mouth until blood was coming out so as not to laugh outwardly at my own mistake.

The next thing that happened was at our season opening game played at Sevierville High School. Before the game, all of our players were getting their uniforms on, and I started taking my coaching clothes off as if I were going to play. After removing my coaching clothes, I realized I didn't have any pads or a uniform to put on, so I sheepishly got dressed again in my coaching clothes. This was the first time I had arrived in a locker room where I wasn't playing.

My teaching assignment was one homeroom, two health classes, and one study hall. I treated all of my classes the same as football practices: with discipline.

For some unknown reason, we had a woman teaching two boys' health classes and I was teaching two girls' health classes. I complained about this to no avail. When it came to personal hygiene, I handed out literature to the girls. Some of the girls would try to embarrass me with questions on personal hygiene. I told them to read the pamphlets that were provided for them.

****

At Fulton High, Dr. Newman had strict discipline on school grounds. When a boy did something very bad, he was sent to a coach's office, where the coach offered him a three-day suspension from school or three whacks with a paddle. I never paddled the same boy twice.

The girls were something else. I held one study hall a day in the auditorium with approximately 100 students sitting in every other seat. I wouldn't allow any talking.

My first week at school I caught a girl talking, and I brought her up in front on the stage. My desk was below the stage facing the students. I said to the girl, "Face the curtains, and touch your toes 50 times."

I heard some laughter from the other students, and I turned around to see the girl touching her toes facing away from the students. She had on a short dress, and every time she bent over to touch her toes her bottom, underneath her dress, was showing. I quickly said, "Stop. And face away from the curtains."

Again, I was in a learning phase of my discipline of girls.

****

The second season, 1964, was the start of a winning tradition at Fulton. The team won eight, lost two, and tied one. There were no state playoffs or championship games played in all six seasons that I coached at Fulton, but there were rewarding bowl games.

This year was the start of five bowl appearances. We had some standout football players. There was Bill Justice, quarterback as a junior, on this team. Bill was a great athlete who was also a great basketball player, making All-State. He took a scholarship his senior year at the University of Tennessee in football and basketball. In order to play football and basketball in the NCAA, rules say you have to sign a football scholarship. His freshman year he played defensive back on the freshman team, but that was the last he played football. He went on to be an All-American basketball player at Tennessee.

Ironically enough, the Dallas Cowboys could have had three athletes playing for them from Fulton High School. Ron Widby played quarterback and punted at Fulton High in 1962, where he made All-State in football, basketball, and baseball. He went on a scholarship to University of Tennessee in 1963. He eventually became an All-American punter in football, an All-American basketball player, and an All-American golfer.

D.D. Lewis was an All-State football player at Fulton High, an All-American linebacker at Mississippi State, a Hall of Famer in Mississippi, and a Hall of Famer in Tennessee. He also played linebacker for Dallas Cowboys.

Bill Justice was an All-State in football and basketball at Fulton went on to be All-American basketball player at U.T. He had not played football since his freshman year at U.T. when the Dallas Cowboys football team drafted him in the third round as a defensive back. He didn't play, which left Ron Widby and D.D. Lewis on the Dallas Cowboys football team.

The captains on the 1964 Fulton football team were Ronnie Wiles, a small fast tail back, and Bob Needham, a center.

Bobby Needham, Fulton High Captain
and Steve Colquitt, South High Captain

This team had the first black player, Oscar White, at Fulton. A situation came up when he played a team in East Tennessee. Irwin High School, who had no blacks in their mountainous community. The week prior to our game with them, Rule High School played them. There were several blacks on Rule's team. After the game, the Irwin fans took offense that Rule had several blacks on their team, and they rocked Rule's bus. I called the football coach of Irwin and informed him we had one black on our team, and I wanted police protection. He said that these people up here are crazy, and he couldn't get protection for my player. I told him our coaches and players will protect Oscar, whatever problem that would cause with their fans and at their place.

I confronted Oscar's mom about the situation, asking her whether she wanted him to go and play at Irwin. She made the decision that Oscar wouldn't go. I said to our team that we were going to win this game for Oscar and if we were to lose, the team would walk back to Knoxville, which was about sixty miles. I told the bus driver, "If we lose, go ten miles down the highway, and the players and coaches will get on the bus at that point and travel the trip back to Knoxville." Irwin High's football team was a good team, but we finally came from behind to beat them. After the game, we showered, got dressed, and came out to the visitor's locker room, no bus. The driver had left when we were behind, so I had to send a parent of one of our players in his car to go down the highway and have the bus driver turn around and come pick us up.

Oscar White became a successful officer in the military. He retired from the U.S. Army as a Full Bird Colonel. He had a great tragedy happen in his life. His wife worked in the Pentagon, in Arlington, Virginia, when one of the planes of the 9/11 attack struck the Pentagon, and his wife was killed. Oscar finished parenting his two children. Both kids earned their graduate degrees.

The 1965 season, my third season, was a great winning season, with eight wins and three losses. It was the year we built and played in our own stadium. Fulton was the only school in the Knoxville area that didn't have its own stadium. Before this year we played our home games at Knoxville Municipal Stadium, Evans-Collins Field. After building the stadium at Fulton, the next four years that I was coaching there, we never lost a home game. This season, we won the Knoxville Football League Championship, and I was honored by the Knoxville Quarterback Club as the Knoxville Football League Coach of the Year.

Building our stadium was a story in itself. We had to raise much of the money ourselves. I heard stories why we could not have a stadium. The main reason I heard was that St. Mary's

Hospital, on the same block, would not allow the stadium because of the noise factor at the games. It would interfere with the hospital's quiet zone. I said, "Let's build it and see who complains." I then involved Cas Walker, who was on the City Council, owned a chain of grocery stores, had his own newspaper, *The Watch Dog,* and had his own T.V. show twice a day on three channels. He basically ran the city at that time. I went on his T.V. show at 6:00 in the mornings, before I went to teach at Fulton. This went on every morning for one week. During the show we were explaining our project and asking people to support it. After we were off the air, Cas would call the people who supplied his stores with their products. He didn't ask them what they could afford to give for the stadium project. He knew how much money he spent for their products and he told each of them the amount they were to give.

Cas said to me, "Coach, if you don't raise enough the city will have to come up with the money to pay it off."

Back at the school, the students sold cookies and candies to support this project. We also got the reserve Marines to level the field with their bulldozers. Coach Jerry Scott, an assistant football coach, was a reserve officer in the Marines. The physical education classes at Fulton were lined up across the field to pick up the many rocks left by the bulldozers. It turned out that the whole community got involved. It made the community come together, taking great pride at Fulton High. I then started the Fulton High Booster Club.

We had many fine athletes that contributed to the success of this winning `65 season. There were several players that made the All-Knoxville Football League All-Stars: David Smith, our quarterback, who earned a football scholarship to Mississippi State; Jerry Russell, our tackle, who became a Hall of Fame football player at Emory and Henry College and went on to get his Doctorate Degree from Vanderbilt and later become my mentor and pastor at Fairview Methodist Church in Maryville, Tennessee; his brother, Jim Russell, who played end and was our punter; and Marshall Walker, a great linebacker. The other All-Star on the team was John Pace. We finished the season playing in the Jaycee Bowl.

The 1966 team, my fourth season, was the start of the endearment name, "The Mighty Mites." This was because of the thirty-man football roster. The average weight was 150 pounds per man. We had two tackles: Doug Young, 128 pounds and Bobby Huffarer, 138 pounds. The offensive and defensive back was Troy Jones, 121 pounds, and the end and defensive back was Warren Wade, 110 pounds. The Mighty Mites had 8 wins and 3 losses. The All-Knoxville football league All-Stars from this team were: David Smith, quarterback, who had a scholarship to Mississippi State; and Billy Wilson, linebacker, who went to Carson Newman on scholarship and made All-American.

The 1967 season, my fifth year, "The Mighty Mites" became champions of the Knoxville football league with 10 wins, 0 losses and 1 tie. We played in the Optimist Bowl versus Morristown. We won 27–6. This was the only Knoxville team to ever beat Oak Ridge. This game was remembered by the hit of Jackie Walker, lineman of the year, on Oak Ridge's fine All-State tailback, Danny Sutton. The hit was heard throughout the stadium with the fans being quiet for the concern of the Oak Ridge player. He was unconscious and taken to St. Mary's Hospital. He later completely recovered. We had many all-stars on this undefeated team. All Knoxville football All-Stars: Larry Brock, our quarterback; Jackie Walker, also East Tennessee and All-State and Tennessee Hall of Fame; Skipper Bean, our linebacker and running back; Butch

Sprain, our offensive center and defensive guard, and he also made All-East Tennessee; and David Mizes, our offensive and defensive tackle. I've always admired players, who through their effort and desire to win, rose far above their ability to become a champion. We had many on this undefeated team. Herb Newton, a tackle on this team, won the most improved player. I received another Coach of the Year award. Later, this team was recognized as the only team at Fulton to be undefeated in 56 years.

My 6th and final season at Fulton High School, 1968, was another fine winning season. We went to our fifth bowl game, The Strawberry Bowl, in Dayton, Tennessee. This record of five bowl games in a row was unmatched by any East Tennessee team. Again we had many stars on this team: Larry Brock, quarterback; Randy Wood, end; Gary Raley, back; Ed Taylor, back; Vince Ingle, back; and Butch Sprain, lineman.

After the '68 season was over, and I was working out the 1969 team on weight machines, I got a call from the head football coach at University of Tennessee, Doug Dickey, asking if I could come over to his office to talk to him. I said I couldn't because I was working out my football players in weights. He said he would come over to Fulton so we could talk. I said, "Fine, come to the back of the building, and I'll have a manager meet you."

When he arrived, the manager came running in and said Coach Dickey was outside in a big limousine and for me to come out to the car. I put someone in charge of the weight machine and I went outside to speak to him. He said, "Get in the car, and we'll talk for a minute." He parked the car and started the conversation saying, "How would you like coaching the linebackers for me?" I told him that this offer was a surprise to me. I asked what would I be making and he said a certain amount.

I answered, "I have five jobs making $25,000 a year, and I would have to have this much to make a living for my family." The jobs were: 1. Teaching; 2. Coaching; 3. Salesman at Sears and Roebuck; 4. Refereeing recreational basketball for City of Knoxville; 5. Playing Semi-Pro Football. He said he would let me know if he could get that salary for me, and I said I would also check with my family and my assistant coaches at Fulton to see whether I should make the move. He got back to me and said he got the salary I was asking for. I took the job of coaching the linebackers at University of Tennessee and the off-season weight program, which they never had at U.T.

Coach Herzbrun – Coach Black – Coach Beam

In summarizing my tenure at Fulton High School, the comradeship we coaches had for one another (Buddy Beam, Jerry Scott, Bobby Fry, Dickie Sharp, Bob Black, Mike LaSorsa, and their families) was the highlight of my life.

These guys were all quality people, coaches, great teachers, and they demanded a lot from the players they coached. That's why we were winners. My motto of "Run with the champions, you become a champion," derived at Fulton High School.

I am most proud of all the players we had the privilege of coaching. They learned in football and life, when you get knocked down, you get back up. All the players that played for us became successful in their life endeavors. They have learned the price to pay to be a champion.

SALESMAN

Sears and Roebuck was very good to me. They put me in the department that was in season for the item that I was to sell. Teaching with a Master's Degree and coaching at that time was difficult to make a good living for a family.

I looked and found supporting jobs that helped my income. The salesman job at Sears was a very tiring and demanding one. We worked on straight commission. If you didn't sell, you couldn't make a living. But if you sold, you would make a very good living.

One summer, for two months they put me in air-conditioners and freezer department. The department had six salesmen all working twelve hours a day, six days a week. No one took a food or bathroom break. If you took a break it could cost you an average $50 a break. I was making $1000 a week.

The largest trophy I ever got was at Sears, and it was for selling more in one month than any salesman at any Sears store in the US.

When a buyer came into our department, a salesman would attack him to make him his customer. Then he had to close the sale quickly in order to take on another customer. There were so many customers coming in, and it seemed like we were clerking. The store opened at 10 a.m. and closed at 10 p.m.

After work, the salesmen would go to the nearby Blue Circle hamburger restaurant and get about 10 to 12 small hamburgers and take them across the street to a beer joint, called the Corner Grill. We would wash the little hamburgers down with a couple beers. We would get home about 11:30 p.m. and wake up at 7 a.m. Each day was the same routine.

In the winter, for two weeks during Christmas break from school, I worked at Sears in the TV and radio department. It was the same routine as I had in the summer, again with straight commission.

We had several TVs on display in the department with their pictures on. This farmer in his bib overalls squatted in front of the largest and most expensive, combination TV, radio and record player we had. No one would wait on him, afraid they would lose a legitimate customer ready to buy. Finally, I confronted the farmer to get him out of the way.

I said, "That's a great TV; let me write that up for you." I wrote it up and took him off to the credit department and left him in line to be waited on, and I went back to the department.

All the salesmen were laughing at me for taking time to wait on him and walking him back to credit. I said, "Was there anything sold? No!"

The farmer came back from the credit department, fuming. I said, "What's wrong?"

He said, "They wouldn't give me credit to buy the TV." The other salesmen were snickering.

I said to the farmer, "The hell with them, just pay for it." He reached in the open side of his bib overalls and pulled out a wad of big bills. He said, "My tobacco just came in and paid me off." He then asked, "Can I take it with me tonight?"

I said, "Do you have a truck?"

He said, "Yeah."

I asked, "Where do you live?"

He said, "Briceville." I took his money and wrote the ticket on the most expensive TV we had. As I was finishing up the ticket, with all the other salesmen watching and listening to what was going on, the farmer said, "We hope to have electricity within six months to a year in Briceville."

I didn't know how to answer, so I said, "But what a beautiful piece of furniture you'll have until you get electricity in the mountains of Briceville, Tennessee."

The other TV salesman told the story to every salesman throughout the store and probably to everyone they knew. The story went to all the Sears and Roebuck stores throughout the country, that I sold the most expensive television set that Sears had to a man without electricity.

Another incident happened during the summer time when I was working at Sears. One morning while I was still in bed, my wife came in and frantically said, "Get up and come outside quickly. There's a snake in the yard." I got dressed and came outside. There was a neighbor, who was a nurse, standing next to my wife and both of them were looking at this large snake which had come from under the woodpile.

I don't like snakes, so I was just standing there with them observing it. The neighbor said, with great confidence, to me: "Pick it up, it's not poisonous."

I picked the snake up close to the head ... but not close enough ... and it whipped its head around and quickly struck my hand with a two-fang bite. I threw the snake in the air and it went back under the woodpile. I said, "Thank God it wasn't poisonous."

The confident neighbor now said, "I'm not sure it wasn't poisonous." So I went to Knoxville to our Fulton High School football team doctor, Dr. Burkhart. I told him the story, he gave me a tetanus shot, and we called the poison control at University of Tennessee.

I was talking to a woman there, and she said, "Describe the snake." I said it was grey on top and had yellow with black X's underneath. She said, "That snake isn't in this part of the country."

I said, "I observed this snake for a long time before I picked it up." Then I asked, "If the snake *was* in this part of the country, was it poisonous?" She said, "Very poisonous."

I then asked, "How will I know I have been poisoned?"

She said, "You will be very sick."

I told her, "I am so nervous right now, I feel sick." I went on to work at Sears, but that whole afternoon I couldn't sell a thing; I was wondering if I was sick. So, I went home. Thankfully, I lived.

Another extra paying job I had, while working at Sears, was playing football on Saturdays during the summer months for the semi-pro team, making a salary of $150 a game. We practiced one night during the week.

I went to the manager of the air conditioners and freezers department where I worked. His name was Charlie Cross, a friend of mine, and I asked him to go along with a scheme I was going to pull off with the remaining salesmen in the department. I told them, "If each of you give me $50 every Tuesday evening, I will leave the floor." I said, "Charlie is going to do it." I used him as an incentive for the rest of the salesmen. Charlie, of course, didn't pay anything. They all said they would do it. Every Tuesday, I marked off each salesman's name as he paid me. I made an extra $200 a week. By my playing football on Saturdays and practicing on Tuesdays, that took me off the sales floor, so the other salesmen made more money. They were happy.

SEMI-PRO FOOTBALL

The Semi-Pro, Southern Football League was made up of ex-players who played football in high school, college (over eight players from the University of Tennessee), and the pros. All were being paid to play. The games were played in Municipal Stadiums throughout the south. Our team was the Knoxville Bears, and in 1966, the team was called the Knoxville SOKs. We played our home games in the Knoxville Municipal Stadium, called Evans-Collins Stadium. The teams were coached by ex-Tennessee Football players: Bert Rechichar, Head Coach`64 and `65, who played many years in the NFL; Gordon Polofsky, Head Coach `66, who was also on the '51 National Championship team and also played pro for the Chicago Cardinals; and Ray Elkas, who was on the Tennessee 1949 team. I played linebacker and was captain all three years, `64, `65, and `66. I received the Knoxville Journal Outstanding Player Award in 1964. We had good teams, and we won 90% of our games and two league championships.

Many interesting things happened while I was playing for the Bears and SOKs. Our `66 SOK's team played the Jacksonville,

Florida team. We took the same old private plane. This plane looked like a vintage plane around the Second World War era. The fuselage had patches of metal on it and the pilot was an older man; we kidded with him calling him Eddy, in reference to the old pilot Eddie Rickenbacker.

During a trip coming back from Jacksonville, an incident occurred. Oil started streaking across the right side windows of the plane. The cockpit door was always open.

We called out to Eddie, "We have a problem. Oil is streaking across the windows on the right side of the plane." Just as we were telling him this news, a big red light began flashing on the dash of the plane. Eddie got out this thick manual and started thumbing through it. The players then got real quiet and put on their seatbelts.

Eddie landed the plane at the Atlanta Airport and taxied to a nearby hanger. The players stayed aboard the plane while it was being looked at and was getting oil. The coaches got off and finally came back with two cases of beer, and they went back on a commercial flight to Knoxville. We took off to Knoxville in the same old plane. The team relied on me, the captain, to talk to the coaches. They weren't ever going on that old plane again. The next away games, we took a different, newer, private plane.

Early in this '66 SOK's season, there was a brawl on the field by the players of the Knoxville and the Chattanooga teams. During the brawl, the Head Coach of Chattanooga picked up a metal chair and threw it at our players. If it had hit one of our players, it could have killed him. The fight was eventually stopped. We finished the game, and we won.

Three games later, this same coach from Chattanooga was now playing quarterback for the Birmingham football team. Our Head Coach, Gordon Polofsky, said "Whoever gets him out of the game, I'll pay him $25.00." I tackled him on the sideline and injured his collarbone. He left the game and after the game he had his arm in a sling. I never got paid. Gordon and I were good friends, then and many years later. In fact, forty-five years later, I was still asking for the $25.00 he owed me. His answer would always be the same: "It's in the mail."

Two players that played for the SOKs, also coached with me at Fulton High School: Mike LaSorsa who was football captain at UT in 1960; and Bob Black, who was an All-American at Carson Newman. Two other players who both played tackle with me on the 1957 team at UT were my best friends, Frank Kolinsky and Jim Smelcher. The four of us, in our later years ran around with each other along with our wives. Both Frank and Mike died in their late 70's, along with our coaches from the Knoxville SOKs, Gordon Polofsky and Ray Elkas, who also were my great friends. Life for me, at eighty years old, is getting lonely.

That game in the '66 season, with the plane incident, was played in Jacksonville, FL, at the stadium where the Gator Bowl was played. The turf was a thick Bermuda grass. I got my cleats caught in that grass near the end of our game. When I came down from trying to intercept a pass, I broke the small bone, the fibula, in the calf area of my right leg, and I had to leave the game. The fibula bone is the bone that supports you getting on your toes.

In this league, you were paid by the game, and if you didn't play, you didn't get paid. Mike LaSorsa, besides playing end for us, was our team trainer. The next week in order to try to help me to play, Mike devised a splint. He took a tin can, both ends open, and taped it around my calf. I ran out on the field and fell flat on my face. I didn't get paid.

The following week I had to play, so Mike put the same can around my calf. This time he added inside the can two thin boards to make it fit more snugly to my calf for more support. I played this game, and during the game, I went up to intercept a pass and forgot about my right leg and came down on it, causing great pain. I threw the ball on the ground, because of the pain.

There were only two more games in this season, in which I wrapped the calf area with an elastic wrap for support. It worked, and I played okay.

University of Tennessee, Coaching

Doug Dickey, Head Football Coach at the University of Tennessee, asked me to be the linebacker coach and strength coach at U.T. I never applied for this job. Coach Dickey had a lot of courage asking me, a high school coach, to coach at the university level. Listed below are the results of Coach Dickey's decision to hire me:

1. 1969 through 1976 Defensive Linebacker Coach and Strength Coach
2. 1969 S.E.C. Champions (under Coach Dickey)
3. Bowl Games I coached while at U.T.:
    a. 1969 Gator Bowl (under Coach Dickey)
    b. 1970 Sugar Bowl (under Coach Bill Battle)
    c. 1971 Liberty Bowl (under Coach Bill Battle)
    d. 1972 Astro-Blue Bonnet Bowl (under Coach Bill Battle)
    e. 1973 Gator Bowl (under Coach Bill Battle)

f. 1974 Liberty Bowl (under Coach Bill Battle)
4. Coached All-American and South Eastern Conference, Linebackers:
   a. Steve Kiner – 1969 All-American, All-SEC, Tennessee Hall of Fame, Butkus Award (top linebacker in the country), Inducted into the National Collegiate Hall of Fame. Played in the NFL, Dallas Cowboys
   b. Jack Reynolds - 1969 All-American, All SEC, Tennessee Hall of Fame, Played in the NFL, Los Angeles Rams and San Francisco 49ers. Both World Champions, All-Pro
   c. Jackie Walker – 1969 Sophomore, All-American, 1970 and 1971 All-American, Tennessee Hall of Fame, Signed with San Francisco 49ers
   d. Ray Nettles – 1971 All-SEC, All-American. Drafted by Miami, All-Pro, Canadian League, Top Defensive Player of the Year, Canada, Played for British Columbia
   e. Jamie Rotella – 1972 All-SEC, All-American, Butkus Award (Top Linebacker in the Country), Tennessee Hall of Fame, Drafted Baltimore, Played in Canada at both Calvary and Hamilton
   f. Art Reynolds – 1973 All-SEC, played pro in the World Football League (New York Stars)
   g. Andy Spiva – 1976 All-SEC, Player in the NFL, Atlanta Falcons
5. Wrote Book – *The Making of an All American Linebacker*, 1973

Some of my memories from my eight years of coaching linebackers at U.T. started in my first year, 1969. I inherited the All-American Linebacker, Steve Kiner, and another who in 1969 would be All-American Linebacker, Jack Reynolds. These two linebackers were at Tennessee before I was hired. Coach Dickey's advice to me was, "Steve Kiner and Jack Reynolds are good linebackers, don't screw them up." I added another great linebacker that season, Jackie Walker, who I had coached at Fulton High School two years prior to the '69 season. Jackie, in his first year of me coaching him at U.T., made sophomore All-American.

The attributes I looked for during recruiting, particularly linebackers, were in this order of importance:

1. Aggressiveness
2. Quickness
3. Speed
4. Size or strength.

All the SEC and All-American linebackers I coached had the first two attributes: aggressiveness and quickness. Steve Kiner probably was the closest linebacker I coached to having all four of these attributes. Kiner made All-American his junior year before I got to U.T. Reynolds became an All-American in '69. He was the best tackler of all the linebackers I coached. Once he made contact with a ball carrier, he never got away. Jackie Walker made sophomore All-American and was the most explosive hitter I ever coached. I felt I was privileged to have coached him in high school and his three years in college. So in 1969, I had three All-American linebackers and we won the SEC.

We had some other outstanding athletes on that championship team. On offense we had: Bobby Scott (quarterback), Curt Watson (running back), and Chip Kell (lineman). On defense we had: Bill Young (safety), Tim Priest (safety), and Herman Weaver (punter).

The only loss during the season was to Ole Miss. Their quarterback was Archie Manning. Many years later, I met his son, Peyton Manning, who was only a sophomore at U.T. We were at a funeral together and I introduced myself to him "You are the second best quarterback I have ever seen; your dad was the first."

We played in the Gator Bowl that year versus a good Florida team. We lost 14 to 13. They had two impact players on their team: John Reeves, their quarterback, and a great receiver, Carlos Alvarez. Our record for the 1969 season was nine wins, two losses. Coach Dickey resigned from U.T. to coach the next season at Florida.

During my second and third years coaching at U.T., we achieved some defensive records that still stand, going on 44 years. The defensive secondary coaches those two years were Buddy Bennett, 1970, and Gary Wyatt, 1971. Again, I had in those years, three All-American linebackers: Jackie Walker `70 and `71; Jamie Rotella `72; and Ray Nettles `72.

These are the NCAA defensive records for those seasons:

1970
- Interceptions – 36
- Fumble Recoveries – 21
- Total Turnovers – 57

1971
- Touchdown on Interceptions – 6
- Interceptions – 25 (for 782 yards)
- Average yardage per Interceptions – 33.3 yards
- Total Interceptions for two years – 61

Jackie Walker (a linebacker) tied Jake Scott, a defensive back from Georgia, for scoring in their college careers, five touchdowns, on defense.

The record for 1970 was eleven wins and one loss. We played in the Sugar Bowl versus Air Force. We won 34–13. Air Force, at game time, was favored to win. They had an All-American receiver Ernie Jennings. Some of U.T.'s star offensive players were: Bobby Scott (quarterback), Curt Watson (tailback), and Chip Kell (center) and an All-American, Lester McLean. U.T.'s star defensive players were: Bobby Majors (safety) and an All-American, Tim Priest (strong safety).

The record for 1971 was ten wins and two losses. We played in the Liberty Bowl versus Arkansas; we won 14–13. The stars of this U.T. team were: Eddie Brown (All-American, played in the NFL, Los Angeles and Washington), Bobby Majors (All-American), Tim Towns, Conrad Graham, George Hunt (kicker). A big game that season was against 5th ranked Penn State, coached by Joe Paterno. We won 31 to 11. They had two great running backs, Lydell Mitchell and Franco Harris. Playing defense for them was John Cappelleti, who in a later season became the running back and won the Heisman trophy. Bobby Majors, a defensive safety for Tennessee, was our punt and kickoff returner. He had an All-American day; 151 yards total on the three punt returns and one kickoff return.

In 1972, my fourth season, our record was ten wins, two losses, and we played the Blue Bonnet Bowl versus L.S.U. We won 24 to 17. L.S.U. had an All-American quarterback, Bert Jones. This '72 season was the first night game ever played at Neyland Stadium. We played 5th ranked Penn State under the lights. We won 28 to 21. The linebackers, this season, were: Jamie Rotella,

All-American and Dick Butkus Award winner (the top linebacker in the country); Eddie Wilson; and Art Reynolds. We had six All-Americans on this team: Condredge Holloway (quarterback, one of the greatest athletes I have ever known); Jamie Rotella (linebacker); Eddie Brown (safety); Bill Emondorfer (guard); Ricky Townsend (kicker); and Neal Clabo (punter).

Other great players on this team were: Robert Pulliam (defensive tackle); Carl Johnson (defensive end); Ken Lambert (defensive end); David Allen (defensive back); Conrad Graham (defensive back and All-SEC); and Tim Townes (safety). This team had two walk-ons that made a great impact on our winning season: Art Reynolds and Tim Townes.

One of my favorite linebackers was Art Reynolds because he came so far with his physical attributes. Art came to U.T. from Cincinnati, Ohio, as a walk-on (no scholarship). He was the brother of Jack Reynolds, an All-American at UT.

Art showed up as a freshman football player, weighing approximately 155 pounds, and when tested in the forty-yard dash, he ran a slow 5.3 seconds. Neither of those statistics would let him play linebacker on any level, or be a contributor. His junior year, we tested our players when they came back from summer at their home to see if they came back in shape for the season. Art came back weighing 205 pounds and in a timed forty-yard sprint he ran 4.8 seconds.

There was a test to run for twelve minutes on the Tom Black track where we would record their time when they came across the finish line. The whole team took off, pacing themselves for the twelve minute run. Art took off full speed, and the coaches, including me, wondered if he knew that they were going to run for twelve minutes. He kept his fast pace up the entire run. After a

103

while he passed almost everyone by one lap, and then on the last lap he passed some slower runners twice. I was scared he might die.

He came across the finish line still running at a fast pace. He didn't fall down, and I was so amazed I grabbed him and said, "Art, how did you do it?"

His answer was that he wanted to be number one. I knew I had a winner.

Coach Battle, head coach, several days later in a meeting asked who my linebackers would be and I answered, "Jamie Rotella, strong side linebacker, Eddie Wilson, weak side linebacker, and Art Reynolds in the middle."

Coach Battle said, "Art is a walk-on."

I said, "He won't let anyone beat him out. Give him a scholarship." Art went on to be a significant force on our defense. After graduation, he played pro-football in the World Football League.

My fifth season, 1973, we had eight wins and four losses. We went to the Gator Bowl versus Texas Tech. We lost 19-28. My three linebackers were: Art Reynolds, Hank Walters, and Eddie Wilson.

Art Reynolds, who made All-SEC, intercepted a pass against Memphis State and ran it ninety-six yards for a touchdown. Some other great players on this team were: Condredge Holloway, who was All-American and received the top offensive player award for several years in Canada; Haskel Standback, running back; Tommy West, tight-end; Eddie Brown, who was All American and played in the NFL (Los Angeles and Washington).

Coach Herzbrun explaining that the ear hole in the helmet
is not there to blow in the running back's ear
before you hit him.

The only time in my whole coaching career that I used a key to determine which direction the offense was going to run the football was when we were playing Kentucky. They were running the veer offense with the top running back in the SEC, Sonny Collins, and with another great back Doug Kotar, who, after playing at Kentucky, played in the NFL with the New York Giants. They moved a big, fast tight end to quarterback in order to have three good running backs in the backfield.

I was watching many films of teams they played that year. I discovered their key habits for certain play calls, for which they were going to run the ball. For example, when the half back Kotar would dive straightforward, his elbow was far in front of his knee before the play started, and when he was to pull parallel to the line, his elbow was next to his knee before the play. That told me which direction they were going to run the ball.

My key discovery was over 95% correct. I called Art in the office and told him the key and then to call "Rip" for right or "Liz" for left for the direction they were going to run the ball. I moved the linebackers up on the line of scrimmage, and when the call was made, they took on the blocker keeping the arm free to the side called. That gave us seven men on the line of scrimmage, each having a gap to control on the side in which they were going to run the ball. We won the game 16 to 14. I was praying throughout the game that they wouldn't take Kotar out of the game because that would have made our key obsolete.

The week before we played Kentucky, I told Art that the center he was playing against was All-SEC and outweighed him by seventy pounds or more. On the first play of the game, Art got knocked back three yards by the center. I took him out of the game and put in Steve Pool. I said to Art, on the sideline, "If you can't whip him, we're going to lose." I put Art back in. He was only out one play. He whipped that guy the rest of the game (it's hard to lose a battle if you won't let the other guy win).

****

At the end of the 1973 season, I wrote a book titled *The Making of an All American Linebacker*. It was a manual for coaches about our successful defensive scheme, particularly linebacker play, and also our weightlifting program at UT. I sold out of this book three times: two were softbacks, and one was hardback.

There were several pages I was particularly proud of: *Building Self-Confidence and a Winning Attitude*, and *My Theory of Coaching Linebackers*. I'm including excerpts from both.

106

Building Self-Confidence and a Winning Attitude

When two teams are roughly equivalent in ability, size and speed, when they both are the products of technically competent coaching -- which wins? Invariably it's the team with that almost indefinable something called poise. And poise is the subtle outward show of inbred confidence.

This positive mental attitude, the most important asset a team can possess, more surely determines success than does raw aptitude. The team that knows it will win seems to make the breaks on which it capitalizes. Driving opportunism is born of ingrained confidence.

The mental, emotional, and physical condition of a team is a result of the attitude it develops. Since attitudes are nothing more than habits of thought, like all habits, they can be acquired.

All positive habits must first be instilled in the players as individuals. Their motivation is pride. And pride is the catalyst that transforms a group of individuals, with all their diversity, into a working unit -- an invincible team. From unquenchable personal desire, based on disciplined self-confidence, there arises an aura that envelops and molds the team.

An athlete is either master or victim of his attitude. Mastery produces a positive self-image. Mastery comes only with practice -- and more practice -- which is the repetition that breeds confidence and poise.

Such confidence means acknowledging one's talent, believing in one's learned abilities; knowing that maximum effort certifies victory and fearing no one.

This is the ultimate in athletic commitment. Nothing else - nothing less - will do. Healthy pride is at stake.

Any player who in his heart is satisfied with less than the best that is in him will end up with less than the best. And second-best is WORSE. If he is willing to accept himself while playing only half the plays in a game, rather than each play as if it were the only play of the game, he will win half his battles, and he will emerge only half alive. If he loses all his battles, and knowledge of his fate does not kill him, he is already dead.

Only the winner knows what it is to be really alive. This exhilaration is more than mere compensation for all the drudgery, all the toil. It is the pinnacle of self-fulfillment. It is pure achievement, gratifyingly earned and justly enjoyed.

My Theory of Coaching Linebackers

✓ First of all, I feel players expect and respect discipline; but they all have different reactions and take different handling. Coach through your personality, not what you've seen someone else say or do. Players will see through anything but you. Give a reason for everything taught so they will see the need for the material.

✓ Teach by repetition but keep training periods short. Three plays run at full speed are better than ten plays run at half speed. Don't teach incorrect practice; remember -- full speed all the way, but not for so long that the players must pace themselves. Strive for perfection.

✓ Make the drills competitive and encourage enthusiasm. Have fun, get a laugh, but not at someone's expense, unless it is your own.

✓ Help players to get the overall picture of defense so they can do their job better. Work hard to win; the harder you work, the harder it is to surrender. E. N. Stewart says that *"victory goes to the team who suffers the most and endures the longest."* Encourage second effort; play each play as if it were the only play.

✓ Players must believe that they are perfectly conditioned, mentally and physically, and especially in condition superior to their opponents.

✓ Play a lot of ball players whenever possible -- You will bring about better practices if your players realize that there is a chance to be recognized on game day. When something is done well, congratulate and try to encourage, rather than discourage through negative or indifferent responses.

✓ As to the coach-player relationship, whenever the player has a problem, encourage him to come to see you -- the door is always open. Let him know you care about him - not only for his football talents, but as a complete individual.

✓ Most of all encourage a burning desire to excel, regardless of the endeavor.

My sixth season, 1974, we had seven wins and three losses. We played in the Liberty Bowl versus a good Maryland team. We won 7-3. They had a great defense tackle, Randy White, who later became an All-Pro for the Dallas Cowboys. My linebackers were: Andy Spiva, a sophomore, All-SEC in 1976, who went on to play for Atlanta in the NFL, (he was killed in a car accident while he was with Atlanta Falcons); Hank Walters; and Steve Pool. We had four All-Americans on this team: Condridge Holloway, quarterback, played pro in Canada; Stanley Morgan, All-American in 1975, who also had a great NFL career with New England;

Larry Seivers, receiver, with the greatest hands I had ever seen; and our kicker, Ricky Townsend. Some other fine football players on that team were: Paul Carruthers; Mickey Marvin, offensive tackle; and Ron McCartney, defensive end, All-SEC, and he played for San Francisco 49ers.

My seventh season, 1975, we had seven wins and five losses in a twelve game season. The last game was against Hawaii. We won 28-6. My linebackers were: Andy Spiva, a junior; Steve Pool; and Hank Walters.

My eighth and final season, 1976, was a winning season with six wins and five losses. I still had a good linebacker, senior Andy Spiva, Greg Jones, and Craig Puki. This season was not up to the standards of Tennessee football. So Bill Battle and our whole staff were let go. Assistant coaches in those days did not have contracts.

We had lost to Alabama (Bear Bryant) five years in a row after beating them five years in a row. In reality, Johnny Majors, a Tennessee hero and a fine coach, had just won the National Championship at Pittsburgh and the Athletic Board wanted him back in Tennessee. Johnny and I played together on the 1956 team, which was SEC champ and number two in the nation. We were always close friends, then and now. When Johnny took the Tennessee job, I was still working in Tennessee.

I set up the top recruits in the Atlanta, Georgia area for Johnny to come by in order to meet and talk to them. Johnny was acting uncomfortable around me. I told him that I understood the situation and that he had to take care of his coaches who helped him win the National Championship. The NCAA, at that time, would only allow three offensive coaches and three defensive coaches. I told him I would make the same decision he would have to make. After that he seemed relieved.

110

In my last season, 1976, I had a disappointment that I have always remembered. I have always had a competitive spirit whether playing or coaching. A situation came up when we were to play Memphis State. They had great success offensively running the veer offense. The week prior to the game, I devised an unorthodox defense as we were having a difficult time stopping the veer. We could use this defense as a change-up. We practiced it during the week. Larry Jones was the defensive coordinator, who called our defensive plays from the press box down to me on the field. Then I would signal it into Andy Spiva to call in the huddle. The first and part of the second quarter, Memphis was running all over us.

During the end of the second quarter, instead of signaling in the defense, Coach Jones was calling down to me. I signaled the unorthodox defense to Spiva on the field. We stopped them dead. I called it intermittently the rest of the second quarter. We came in at half-time and Coach Battle came up to the defensive coaches and asked how we were going to stop Memphis State the second half. I said we would call the unorthodox defense. Coach Battle said that they will catch on and counter it. I said that at least they would have to do something different.

The second half, I signaled our basic defense called by Coach Jones, and again they were running through us. The rest of the game in certain situations I signaled in the unorthodox defense, over the basic defense called down to me. We won 21-14. I knew if we hadn't won, I would have been fired on the spot. Neither Coach Jones nor Coach Battle came up to me to say, "Thanks."

In summarizing my eight years at Tennessee, I was privileged to coach groups of linebackers who were willing to pay the price to be winners.

111

OVERTIME

BUSINESS

After leaving my coaching position at University of Tennessee, I had my family to look after. My son Eric was in Business College at UT. My daughter, Yvette, was dancing ballet professionally. My wife, Wilma, at this point was still a housewife. I really didn't want to move away from where we lived in Blount County, Tennessee. We lived in Alcoa and Louisville. My son graduated from Alcoa High School. We also lived in Maryville. My daughter graduated from Maryville High School. My wife Wilma had graduated from Alcoa High School. All these towns were in Blount County. I was very hesitant to leave this area. I looked at many opportunities coaching in college, and one pro team showed a lot of interest in me coaching there.

I've always thought the mountains and the oceans had to be God's work. They're too massive for man to make. I also enjoyed the four seasons of the year in East Tennessee. I get bored with only a small variance found in all predominantly one-season areas.

I've always said, "Winter appears ugly here in Blount County, only because the other seasons ... Spring, Summer, and Fall ... are so beautiful." We get spoiled. I also wanted to give back to this community what it had afforded to my family.

I approached a friend of mine, and also my CPA, Harold King. We knew each other when he was only a CPA. He said to me, "I'm tired of making money for everyone else. I'm going to invest myself in real estate." He did, and he became very wealthy. When I left coaching, he asked me what I was going to do. I told him I had the idea of opening a health club, and that this community needed one. He said he had some land close to downtown Maryville. I went and looked at it and reported back to Harold. I told him, "It isn't what I think is appealing for a health club."

The county had just completed what they called the Greenbelt in downtown Maryville, and there was a wooded lot on a hill overlooking the newly built walking trails, the lake, and the panoramic view of the Smoky Mountains. The hill was called Parham Hill, which also was where the old armory was located. I came back to Harold and said, "I found the perfect spot for the club."

Together, we approached the Maryville City Council to obtain the land. We told them what we were going to put on the land. Actually there were two parcels of land. Harold was going to put condominiums on the same parcel that I was going to put the club on. He was going to put a high-rise apartment complex on the other parcel. I got up and explained my use for Parham Hill, which was to build a health club that would coincide with the Greenbelt walking trails. Our competition for this land was Blazer Insurance.

We ended up getting the land. That was the start of Olympia Athletic Club. Harold put up the money for the club, which I leased from him and eventually paid off, as well as buying the condos on the same parcel as the club.

I ended up building a large 30,000 square-foot health club. This is my area of expertise. I wrote and administrated conditioning programs for athletes, which I modified to the everyday person, who wanted to get and stay in shape by adding healthy years to their life. I called the health club Olympia Athletic Club. Our motto is, "Add years to your life and life to your years."

I came across the craftsman, Leroy Newlin, almost by accident. I went into a craft store in Maryville, where hanging on a wall was a mirror type window encased in rough sawn hardwood. I was intrigued with this work because I wanted the walls on the inside of the club to be made of rough looking hardwood.

I got the name of the craftsman who built this hardwood-mirrored window. I called Leroy up and asked him to meet with me. I took the drawing I made up and explained that I was going to build a health club with walls inside of hardwood. I asked if he would be interested in supervising and building this club with me. He said, "Let's do it."

We became great friends for many years. When I say I built a club, I mean I designed and physically did the physical labor on it. Leroy, another older gentleman, and I put all the rough sawn hardwood on the walls. I subcontracted out the outside structure and the heating, air conditioning, electric, plumbing, and swimming pool.

I wanted the inside of the rough sawn boards to match the mountain look. I bought discarded hardwood boards from the Veach May Wilson in Alcoa. They used hardwood for building beds for trucks. I got them to plane one side, leaving the other side rough, and then kiln dry all of the wood. We brought over 30,000

117

board feet of hardwood to the club. We sawed and put up the boards throughout the club. We had to shoot nails with the nail gun, in order to penetrate the hard hickory. Old hickory is like steel; it has existed for thirty-seven years in the club and looks the same as when we nailed it up.

At a later date, we bought the land where they had torn down the old armory and we built more condos. Eventually we sold all the condos.

My son Eric had graduated in business from UT and my daughter Yvette came from a professional ballet company. She had been dancing with two different companies: one in Denver, Colorado, and the other in Seattle, Washington. The three of us, along with their mother, Wilma, became equal partners.

The Herzbrun Family

Eric and I managed and sold memberships. Wilma taught Yvette bookkeeping. Both of them did the bookkeeping. Yvette also taught and was in charge of the backbone of the club, aerobics. The club could not have been successful without the whole family dedicating their being to accomplish their responsibilities.

I am so proud of my family and their work ethic. Business is similar to football because sometimes you get knocked down, but the winners get back up. I have a family of winners. We have now been in business thirty-seven years.

****

During this time while we were running the club, several events took place. Johnny Majors, one of my great friends, was inducted into the College Hall of Fame. He invited some of his teammates from Tennessee for dinner at the Waldorf Astoria in New York. I had to make some arrangements at Olympia in order to go. At the last minute, I did go. I made the trip with my good friend Frank Kolinsky, who played tackle next to me during the `56 and `57 seasons at Tennessee.

There were four of us in the same room: me; Frank; another good friend, who also played tackle on those teams, Jim Smelcher; and a wingback, Bob Hibbard. After congregating in the lobby, it was time to go to the room and get dressed for the banquet. I noticed all four of my teammates were putting on tuxedos. I hadn't gotten the word since I had made arrangements to go at the last minute. Frank said, "2000 people are in there in tuxedos and one in a suit."

I said, "I'll go down the block from the hotel and rent one."

Frank said, "I'll go with you."

I go into the tux rental store, and Frank said, "Try on everything." I tried on the coat, vest, pants and shoes. The tux looked great. The shirt was folded and wrapped in the plastic. I told the salesman I have a large neck, 18 1/2 inches, and long arms, thirty-seven inches long.

He said, "It will fit."

Frank said, "Try it on."

I said, "If I unwrap it, how will I carry it back to the hotel?"

The salesman again assured me, "It will fit."

We went back to our room, and I put on the shirt The neck was at least an inch too small for me to be able to button it. So I put the bowtie on and held my head down, so my chin covered the space of the collar behind the tie. The sleeves were short and way up on my forearms. Frank got two white washcloths and pinned them around my wrists, so as to show slightly from beneath the sleeves of my coat. I was walking with my head down, and my chin against my chest, with my arms folded at the elbow, hoping the imperfections of the shirt sizes were not noticeable.

Frank ran into a friend of his from Pittsburgh, and I overheard Frank telling him about coming to New York with me and about both of us being teammates of Johnny Majors. I was a little distance away from Frank and his friend, but I could still hear them speaking. His friends said, referring to me, that I was wearing a nice looking tux ... for a cripple. Frank explained, "He played a lot of football."

Another time, while I was working at Olympia, I was to be inducted into the Greater Washington, D.C., Jewish Sports Hall of Fame in 1998. I invited my friend Frank Kolinsky to drive and accompany me to the banquet in D.C. Johnny Majors made arrangements to be there along with my teammates from Woodrow Wilson High School. My best friend from high school days, Terry Lindsey, arranged to have a luxury room in the hotel in D.C. and a limousine to take Frank and me to the banquet. Terry owns about five automobile dealerships in Virginia near D.C.

Frank and I arrived on Friday evening and I called Terry up to thank him for his generosity of the room and limousine. I asked Terry if he had a sales meeting with all of his sales people on Saturday morning as most dealerships do. When he said yes, I said, "What if Frank and I were to talk on motivation to your sales force?"

He said, "Would you do that?"

I said, "Frank and I would love to do that." There were about fifty salesmen at the meeting from all of his dealerships at the meeting held at his Cadillac dealership. After I was introduced, I gave my talk and near the end of my talk was explaining, "In the 1957 season, Frank and I were the heaviest players on the first string. I came back prior to the season weighing 220 pounds, Frank came back weighing 240 pounds. They put both of us on skim milk and a wedge of lettuce for lunch, during two a day practices, in order to get our weight down. We both ended up playing at 205 pounds." I added, "You got to understand we went both ways then, offensive and defensive."

My introduction of Frank was, "Here's Frank; he still goes both ways." The salesmen laughed, and when Frank got up to talk, his whole brief talk was focused on the fact that he wasn't queer.

I said, "Frank, you really motivated them."

He said, "You son of a bitch."

During the period of our Olympia Athletic Club business, I lived for over ten years on board several boats on the Tennessee River near Knoxville, Tennessee. During that time, I took several trips down river on my cruiser to Chattanooga, Tennessee, 140 miles from where I docked my boat.

One trip was most memorable. I made it with two long lasting friends, Brad and Clara Sayles and their preacher from Friendsville Methodist Church, Wendell Smith. His church is one of the churches where I gave my testimonial. We had only gone down river thirteen miles, and Brad and I were piloting the boat from the fly bridge when Clara nonchalantly approached me and said, "Lonnie, is the water supposed to be above your ankles in the bedroom?"

I quickly put Brad in charge of piloting the boat and rushed down into the stateroom. Sure enough the water was above my ankles. I went back up to the fly bridge and piloted the boat over to a nearby dock. Prior to leaving on our trip, I had had a mechanic check out the drive shaft of the boat and he hadn't tightened a coupling. The bilge pump could not take care of the excessive water. I called up the mechanic and within the hour he arrived by truck. After he went down in the hull and tightened the coupling, we continued our successful trip to Chattanooga.

Years later I moved back to a house on turf.

I was recently asked about my health. I said, "I'm still on the green side of the turf."

Maryville College

In 1977, while I was building Olympia, the head football coach from Maryville College, Jim Jordan, asked if I would help coach the defense and linebackers. I said I would, and took over coordinating the defense and coaching the linebackers. I had three fine linebackers: Tony Ierulli, who later became head coach at Maryville College and then became assistant coach at Carson Newman College; Wayne Dunn, who was small college All-American linebacker and also an All-American wrestler, was inducted into the Blount County Hall of Fame and died several months later; and the third linebacker was Alvin Richmond, a quick explosive linebacker. We almost went to playoffs. We won six and lost two.

For the last three road games, the team went by bus because they were over 400 miles from Maryville. We lost the last two games because the players were tired from the travel. The next to last game was against Rhodes College in Memphis, Tennessee. If we had won that game, we would have been in the playoffs. We lost by a touchdown, 21 to 28.

An embarrassing incident happened during the game with Rhodes College. Our team was on the sideline, facing the fans in the stadium across the field from us. During the game, three drunken students were close to our team's bench, and all that was dividing them from us was a twelve-foot chain-link fence. One of the drunken students was calling out profanity directly at our coaches and players throughout the game, and then he pulled out a big knife and was taunting us by waving it and yelling out profanity. I took as much of his loudmouth as I could stand. I then rushed the tall fence and started to climb the chain link fence telling the drunk with the foul mouth, "I'm going to stick the knife clean up your _____."

When I got close to the top of the fence, one of my linebackers Tony Ierulli was trying to pull me down by pulling on the sweatpants I was wearing. My pants came down to my ankles while I was hanging on the top of the fence. I was wearing only my jock. My whole lower backside (bottom) was facing all the fans on the other side of the field. The three drunken students, including the one with the foul mouth waving the knife, took off running when I got closer to the top of the fence. After the game was over, the president of Rhodes College came over to me and apologized for the drunken students. I thought he was coming over to tell me he loved me, after my pants down exhibition.

After the season, Maryville College didn't have a football banquet lined up for the team, so I said, "We're going to have a football banquet at the Frog." This was a bar in downtown Maryville. It was a real dump. "Invite the cheerleaders."

I didn't announce to the owner, who was also the bartender, we were coming. We arrived, and there was only one drunk in the place. He left. We lined up the tables and chairs in a big "M".

Everyone showed up, and we had our Maryville College football banquet.

I told the owner we were going to have the football banquet here every year; he said, "Hell no!"

HOLY SPIRIT

The most unexpected experience came into my life when D.D. Lewis was to give his testimonial at a small Christian church in Knoxville, Tennessee. The Pastor was Larry Cash, who played football with D.D. at Fulton High School in Knoxville when I was the football coach there. D.D. asked Larry to call me to see if I could be there at the church when he was to give his testimonial. I told Larry I would.

D.D. had finished his long fourteen year career with the Dallas Cowboys in the NFL. He got on drugs, and his life was going downhill, but then Christ came into his life. Through his belief in Christ, he conquered his drug addiction. He talked about his young life in Knoxville, which I already knew. He was always in trouble, and had a tough home life. During his testimonial and the church service itself, I'm not exactly sure what took place, but all I know is I started tearing up, and I came up on the altar, and D.D. and Larry had their arms around me. I knew right then that Christ came into my life. It was wintertime when I walked out of the small church, but the sun was beaming brightly. After that I went to a dozen different Christian churches to find a teacher to explain the Bible to me. I read the Bible from front to back, but I wasn't sure that I understood what I read.

I needed a scholar who knew the Bible and could teach it. I found him at Fairview Methodist Church in Maryville, Tennessee, where I lived. The pastor was Jerry Russell, who I had coached at Fulton High School. I wrote a letter nine months later, after I received a kind letter from D.D. My letter to D.D. was my experience, starting with his testimonial at Larry Cash's church. Here is that letter:

January 4, 2000

Dear D.D.

The biggest day of my life was when you gave your testimonial at Larry Cash's church. That day, May 2, 1999, after hearing you, Christ came into my life. I've always been blessed and had champions surrounding me, persons who were willing to pay the price to win their battles, whether it be in athletics or in life itself. I knew you always had great courage, but on May 2, 1999 when I heard you give your testimonial, I realized you were truly a great, great champion. You had the courage to overcome the adversities that you faced in your life.

The letter you wrote me on December 29, 1999 will always be cherished. It was the best present I could have received, especially on my very first Christmas in my life.

I am being baptized this Sunday, January 9, 2000 at Fairview United Methodist Church in Maryville, Tennessee. I am also joining that church the same day. Interesting enough, the pastor of Fairview Church is Jerry Russell, who I also coached at Fulton

High School. God directed Jerry in the right profession for him - what a great minister. I coached him in football and now he is coaching me in the Holy Spirit - a much more important aspect of life.

D.D., you were always an exceptional person in my life and now you are an inspiration in changing my life, bringing me closer to God through Christ.

I love you.

Lon Herzbrun

Radio Show

Bob Gilbert was director of news operations at UT, a reporter for the local paper, The Daily Times, a reporter for the Associated Press, and longtime friend of mine. He approached me during the same year we opened Olympia Athletic Club about starting a local sports radio show with me live from Olympia. I told him radio broadcasting was not my cup of tea, but if it brought more recognition to the young athletes in Blount County, I would go along with him. So we started the show at the club with one of the local A.M. Radio Stations. The show broadcasted for two hours. It was very successful.

Bob, being with the Associated Press, knew many reporters across the county, as well as sports celebrities, such as: Coach Bear Bryant from Alabama; Joe Paterno from Penn State; and many others with national status who were on the show; some live, and some by phone. Bob and I enjoyed broadcasting the show for thirty-five years. The show was moved in those years to two different locations.

Bob had some health issues and got three local ex-athletes to take over the show: Charlie Puleo, who pitched for the Atlanta Braves; Mike Edwards, an All-American basketball player with UT; and Donnie Moore, a record-setting punter in football at Maryville College. All three of these athletes coached at the same local high school in Blount County, William Blount High School. Charlie Puleo coached baseball; Mike Edwards coached basketball; and Donnie Moore was the athletic director.

The show is now live at a restaurant called Barley's, in downtown Maryville. It is now in its 37th year, the longest-running sports show in Tennessee. Ray Trail, who was a very successful offensive line coach at UT, and I are advertised as legendary coaches. I believe that title has to do more with our age. I guess that's better than ancient coaches. We are part of the show every week.

The Sports Page show has taken on a little different format than before. The emphasis is more on all local sports, which includes UT, Maryville College and all local high schools. Sports in Blount County are very big, mainly because of the two dominant city football teams, constant champions in the state, Alcoa and Maryville. Girls' basketball also has great traditions in Blount County, so the show is well received by the sports fans.

HALL OF FAME AND ACHIEVEMENT AWARDS

All the awards I received, whether Hall of Fame or achievement awards, came to me because of team championships. One man on a team doesn't win championships by himself. You have to surround yourself with coaches and players that have the same burning desire as you to win and are willing to pay the price in practice to finish and be a winner.

It is hard to lose if you won't let someone beat you.

These Halls of Fame and achievement awards were presented to me, but I look upon them as team achievements.

➤ Greater Washington, D.C., Jewish Hall of Fame, 1998
➤ 10th Jocks Hall of Fame, Washington, D.C., 1999
➤ Greater Knoxville Hall of Fame, 2004
➤ Blount County Hall of Fame, 2008
➤ Touchdown Club, Washington, D.C., Outstanding Armed Forces Player of the Year, 1961
➤ Most Valuable, East Coast Interservice Conference, 1961

- Most Valuable, Fort Eustice, 1961
- Charity Bowl, Fort Campbell, Best Lineman, 1960
- Knoxville Quarterback Club, Coach of the Year, 1965
- Knoxville Quarterback Club, Coach of the Year, 1967
- Knoxville Journal Team Player Award, Knoxville Bears, 1964
- City of Knoxville, Proclamation for High School Achievement, 2007
- Salute America Inspiration Award, "There's a winner in you", 2007
- The State of Tennessee, Colonel Aide de Camp Award, (1967 Fulton Falcon), 2007, Governor Phil Bredesen
- House of Representatives Salute Award, (1967 Fulton Falcon), 2007

Awards

A friend once asked me my definition of a champion. Without hesitation, I said, "One who prepares and finishes."

I have always questioned, "Where did I develop this burning desire to win?" After writing this book my answer is, "God."

You can see physical attributes, but to be given a desire to win is an inborn quality that one can't see physically. This quality can be refined into a burning desire to accomplish an objective through repetition ... which is how you get the tool to excel: *confidence.*

133

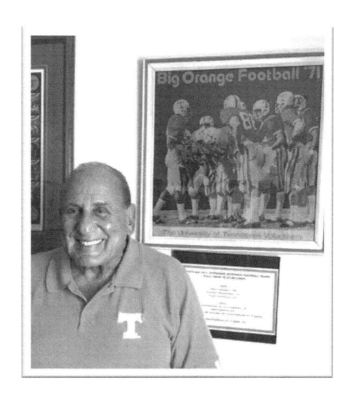

"I INVESTED IN
PEOPLE WHO WERE
WILLING TO PAY
THE ENORMOUS PRICE
TO BE CHAMPIONS"

Lon Herzbrun

EPILOGUE

MOTIVATING RECOGNITION
LETTERS FROM CHAMPIONS IN MY LIFE

Terry Lindsay – A great high school and longtime friend and successful businessman in the Metropolitan, D.C. area. He is the chairman of the Board of Saint Luke Institute and has served on many other civic boards.

This is a letter Terry wrote to Tony Kornheiser, a columnist and national T.V. radio personality from the Greater Washington D.C. area:

"Last week, I was listening to your radio show, at the time you were paying tribute to Mohammed Ali. Much of what was said could apply to Lon Herzbrun – obviously in a much smaller arena. To his friends and teammates in the early 50's, he was the guy!

"Athletically, he dominated the high school scene in football, basketball and baseball. He was and still is a natural born leader totally driven to be the best. When our team was behind in a game

or in tight situations, everyone looked to Lonnie for direction. He always had the right focus, was clear headed and intuitively knew what to do. The coaches looked to Lonnie, asking him, 'What do we do now?' He had that much respect and would always find a way to win!

"Through his ability and the motivation he provided our high school, Woodrow Wilson won city championships in all three major sports in 1952-1953. He constantly pushed those around him to perform beyond their expectations. He demanded 110% effort from everyone in every situation. The results spoke for themselves."

Frank Kolinsky – Played tackle in football, beside me at the University of Tennessee, and was a longtime friend. He headed up a drug and alcohol rehab home in Knoxville, Tennessee, the E. M. Jellinek Center. He also was president for the State of Tennessee Alcohol and Drug Association. He died in 2011.

This is a congratulations letter drafted to me in 2004.

"Lon '64': Congratulations for your being selected into the Knoxville Hall of Fame. I know how proud I will be to see you accept another award.

"Fifty-one years of being around you have made me a better man. The two of us did well on the field, but I know we did even better in life after the game was played.

"I thank God I have a friend, pal, buddy and teammate to be with all these years."

Another letter from Frank:

"Other than athletics, where else can people with different ethnic and religious backgrounds and from different areas in the U.S. become teammates and lifetime best friends?

1. *John Majors – Anglo Saxon, Protestant, Lynchburg, Tennessee*
2. *Lon Herzbrun – Hungarian, Jew, Washington, D.C.*
3. *Jim Smelcher – Part Cherokee Indian, Protestant, Lake City, Tennessee*
4. *Mike LaSorsa – Italian, Catholic, Providence, Rhode Island*
5. *Frank Kolinsky – Russian, Catholic, McKees Rock, Pennsylvania"*

John Majors – A teammate in 1953, `54, `55 and `56 at University of Tennessee. He was All-American, second in the Heisman Trophy (top football player in the nation), National Coach of the Year 1973 and 1976. His team at Pittsburgh University won the national championship in 1976.

A note to me from John "Drum" Majors, The Huntland Hornet:

"To my great friend and wonderful teammate Lon Herzbrun: a true and loyal friend through thick and thin!!"

Jamie Rotella – University of Tennessee Team Captain 1972, All-SEC 1972, All-American `72, in 1977 selected for the Butkus Award (Best Linebacker in College Football) for `72 season at Tennessee. Drafted third round NFL, Played in Canada 1973, `72 Hamilton Tiger Cats, and the Calvary Stampeders in 1975. Inducted into the Tennessee Hall of Fame in 2015.

A letter to me from Rotella:

"You certainly coached a lot of talented linebackers in a short span. While some like Jackie Walker have awesome

athleticism, others like myself, brought mostly desire. Your principles in linebacking and defense overall always put us in a position to win. In following your simple yet extremely effective keys to read, we found ourselves on a collision course with the ball carrier, and that's a fun way to play linebacker! The best visual you gave us was in teaching the art of explosion at the point of contact and comparing it to Hank Aaron striking the baseball. I know Jackie and Ray Nettles mastered that technique because in pregame warm-ups before I became a starter I had to run the ball against them. They literally had me looking out my ear hole.

"You worked us hard but always gave us the positive encouragement it takes to develop a winning attitude. You wanted us to think like winners, and that spirit has carried on with us in life. On behalf of all your former players, thank you, Coach."

D.D. Lewis – Played football for me at Fulton High School, Knoxville, Tennessee. He then played football for Mississippi State where he became an All-American, Mississippi Hall of Fame, and Tennessee Hall of Fame and played fourteen years for The Dallas Cowboys, where he played in five Super Bowls, winning two of them.

He wrote this letter to me:

"The main reason I wanted to write this letter is to tell you how grateful I am that God put you in my life. I've heard it said, 'When the student is ready, the teacher will appear.' You were a positive influence on me at a time when I needed it most.

"Coach, you were one of those people that treated me special. It wasn't hyperbole, it was genuine and I thank you for it. I am sure you've had an important effect on many a young man throughout your coaching career, but it would be hard to find one

you affected more than me. You will always be an exceptional person in my life."

General Westmoreland – I served as a Second Lieutenant with the 101st Airborne under Commander General Westmoreland. He later became Superintendent of West Point and Supreme Commander of the Armed Forces in Vietnam. This is a letter to General Besson, Commandant of the Transportation School at Ft. Eustice, Virginia where I was then stationed, from General Westmoreland when he was Superintendent of West Point:

"Lt. Herzbrun is personally known to me as an outstanding officer, as well as a talented athlete. We are, therefore, most anxious to secure his services to assist in our athletic program, at West Point. He would be a particularly valuable addition to our football coaching staff."

Jake Newton – This is a letter from a junior linebacker in his high school, Christian Academy of Knoxville. Jake is the son of Herb Newton, a champion high school football player, who I had coached at Fulton High School in Knoxville, Tennessee. This letter is written to me as a result of a conversation and a note I had sent to Jake on how to become a great linebacker. He quoted many things we discussed in our conversation and in the note I sent him after I witnessed him playing a football game.

" 'Jake you are a winner!'

#1 'Desire to win each play is not made during that play. It is only exhibited then.'

#2 'To determine to win your game. Play each play like it was the only play of the game! Above all don't worry about the outcome of winning or losing the game. You must think about you winning your very first play!'

#3 'Don't say what you are going to do! Go do it!!!'

#4 'All-state players are made in big games'

"Thank you coach for your wisdom. I will not let you down."

Jake Newton #30

To my children's mother Wilma, to my son, Eric and to my daughter, Yvette: I am very proud of you and hold you in high esteem. Many of my accomplishments were to make you proud of me.

Thanks,

Lonnie - Dad

Additional copies of this book can be ordered through

www.amazon.com

as soft cover or e-book

46616329R00088

Made in the USA
Charleston, SC
21 September 2015